THE TURNAROUND POWER OF THE WORD

DAVID O. OYEDEPO

THE TURNAROUND POWER OF THE WORD

David O. Oyedepo

ISBN 978-978-2905-97-0

Published in Nigeria by

DOMINION PUBLISHING HOUSE

DOMINION PUBLISHING HOUSE

Km 10, Idiroko Road, Canaanland, Ota, Nigeria.

Tel: +234 816 406 0777, +234 909 151 4022

Or visit our website: ***www.dphprints.com***

All Scripture quotations are from the King James Version of the Bible, except otherwise stated.

CONTENTS

Introduction

But the path of the just is as the shining light, that shineth more and more unto the perfect day.

Proverbs 4:18

By redemption, we are destined for turnarounds. The above scripture says, "The path of the just." Who is the just? He is the man who has been justified by Jesus. He is like "the" shining light that shines unto the perfect day. Thus, we are not ordained to be static.

When we do not experience change, we become sources of concern to God. This is because God has sent His Word as a turnaround tool. God's agenda for us is to experience supernatural turnaround at every point in time, in our journey through life. As I have always said, there is nothing small that cannot become big and there is nothing big that cannot get bigger. There is nothing little that cannot become great, and there is nothing great that cannot turn greater. Experiencing a turnaround is not just for downtrodden people that are struggling to find their bearing in life; it is for all of God's people.

Every child of God is entitled to a lifelong turnaround experience. As children of God, we are most privileged to have blessed lives on earth. If those who are not born again are advancing, imagine how much God expects of us. As we behold Him as in a glass (daily), we are changed from glory to glory (2 Corinthians 3:18).

The Word is God's wisdom for our desired turnaround; He upholds all things by the Word of His power. That means, He controls all things through His Word.

> ***Who being the brightness of His glory, and the express image of His person, and upholding all things by the word of His power, when He had by Himself purged our sins, sat down on the right hand of the Majesty on high.***
>
> *Hebrews 1:3*

It is very interesting to know that every turnaround we will ever experience is absolutely by the Word. It is not just by finding the Word but also by engaging it, to bring about an inexplicable experience.

While access to the Word is the heritage of the redeemed, only the spiritual among the saved can access the mystery of the Word. It is one thing to be saved, and another to be spiritual.

> ***But the natural man receiveth not the things of the Spirit of God: for they are foolishness unto him: neither can he know them, because they are spiritually discerned.***
>
> *1 Corinthians 2:14*

The Word is our covenant turnaround tool, and the degree of turnaround testimonies we command is a function of our spiritual insight, depth and understanding.

Through the expositions of the truth in this book, you will come in contact with facts on how to get your own word for a turnaround experience, which will make your life better, richer and happier.

ONE

WHAT IS THE WORD WORTH?

In the beginning was the Word, and the Word was with God, and the Word was God. The same was in the beginning with God. All things were made by him; and without him was not any thing made that was made.

John 1:1-3

The Bible is the most valuable volume of all times. It is the oldest, yet the most current. It is also the most ancient, yet the bestseller of all times. It is the most widely quoted book and its principles still rule most of the civilised societies today. Its content touches all aspects of human existence, and that is what makes it the key to our unending turnarounds.

The Bible is a living force and there is something

unique about it. God's Word is ever reliable, ever dependable, and eternally functional. His Word backs His integrity; therefore, we can count on Him. We can also settle with Him and in turn, experience the working power of the Word.

What we do with the Word largely determines our destiny. That means, it is our value for the Word that defines our destiny. This is because the contents of the Bible are spiritual laws that confer us with dominion in our earthly walk. The light of God's Word does not only enlighten; it also lightens us.

It is written:

> ***In the beginning was the Word, and the Word was with God, and the Word was God.***
>
> ***In him was life; and the life was the light of men.***
>
> ***That was the true Light, which lighteth every man that cometh into the world.***
>
> *John 1:1, 4, 9*

The Word puts us in command of everything, because all things were created by the Word, and everything remains under the command of the Word forever (John 1:3). Therefore, having potentials or skills is not a substitute for gaining command over our desired turnarounds.

We must have the consciousness that the devil is not as powerful as we think he is; rather, it is our ignorance of the dominion we have over him, through the Word, that makes him torment us. This is because our "lightlessness" gives him power. Therefore, when we are lightened, we are free and in charge of all circumstances of life.

One of the most awesome encounters I had in my early Christian life was from Jeremiah 29:11:

> ***For I know the plans I have for you, says the Lord, plans for welfare and not for evil, to give you a future and a hope*** *(Revised Standard Version).*

The Word of the Lord came to me saying: "Your future is in My plan, not your plan." That hit me so much and gave me a greater sense of value for God's plan for my life. I discovered that the plan is packaged in the Bible.

I know that the law is spiritual (Romans 7:14). Thus, the Bible is a spiritual text powered to quicken destinies, and cause them to come alive. In it, we have the power to restore harmony into families and breakthroughs in the place of breakdowns.

Too many people approach the Bible like a motivational or a religious text, where they draw religious principles. That makes them relegated day-in, day-out, because they don't know what it carries. The Bible is the only "charm" that does not lose its potency. The application of God's Word works any day and at anytime.

He said: ***My son, eat thou honey, because it is good; and the honeycomb, which is sweet to thy taste: So shall the knowledge of wisdom be unto thy soul: when thou hast found it, then there shall be a reward, and thy expectation shall not be cut off*** (Proverbs 24:13-14).

Jesus is the wisdom and the power of God, and He is the Word of God. God's Word is also the wisdom of God; thus, the knowledge of the Word of God is like eating honey from the honeycomb. God said that when we eat the Word, there is bound to be a reward because our expectations shall not be cut off.

There is a war-free zone in life. For instance, God gave the Israelites rest round about. Also, Solomon didn't have to fight any war in all the years of his life. With this understanding, we must realise that there is a war-free zone in life, which is only accessible by the wisdom of God encountered in the Word.

Her ways are ways of pleasantness, and all her paths are peace (Proverbs 3:17).

The Bible provides appropriate answers to every question that will ever arise on this earth. Peter said to Jesus: *Master, we have toiled all the night, and have taken nothing: nevertheless at thy word...* (Luke 5:5). When they put the Word to work, it produced a great harvest. The Word works!

We might not know the efficacy of the Word until we begin to put it to work in faith, delightedly, cheerfully, excitedly, lovingly, passionately, zealously and selflessly. This is because the Bible cannot be re-written. We either connect with what is written or we are disconnected from it.

The Spirit Power of the Word

> ***It is the spirit that quickeneth; the flesh profiteth nothing: the words that I speak unto you, they are spirit, and they are life.***
>
> *John 6:63*

God's Word is Spirit and life, and it is able to quicken. Remember, it is "the Spirit that quickeneth" and is able to give life to anything called dead. It can also invigorate everything that is dying. Thus, the Bible enables us to partake of that divine nature of God that gives us dominion over the things that corrupt the world.

By the Word, we become partakers of the divine nature, escaping the corruption that is in the world through lust. It infuses the nature of God into us, and confers us with dominion over everything that is molesting the world (2 Peter 1:4).

Thus, God's Word is Spirit-born, because the Word is a product of the Spirit and like begets like. Therefore, God's Word is Spirit and every statement of Scripture is gathered by the Spirit of God.

It is written: ***And take the helmet of salvation, and the sword of the Spirit, which is the word of God*** (Ephesians 6:17).

Therefore, when we engage the Word, we are engaging the Spirit of God as a standard against the attacks of the enemy. The Spirit of God is our guarantee for victory in every spiritual conflict and when the enemy is defeated, our turnaround is guaranteed (Isaiah 59:19).

It is written: ***Seek ye out of the book of the Lord, and read: no one of these shall fail, none shall want her mate: for my mouth it hath commanded, and his spirit it hath gathered them*** (Isaiah 34:16).

Remember that when the devil tempted Jesus on the mount of temptation, He tackled him with "It is written," and the devil left Him. There is no force against our path of turnaround that will not bow to the right Word, because we encounter the raw power of God from His Word.

God's Word is His power in print and we cannot engage the sword of the Lord and still be grounded. When we engage the Spirit of the Word against the operations of hell, our victory is sure.

Empowerment in the Word

God's Word is self-anointed and it is divinely

empowered. God's power is in His Word (John 6:63). This can be understood particularly when we know that God is omnipotent; which means that He is All-powerful.

> ***In the beginning was the Word, and the Word was with God, and the Word was God.***
>
> *John 1:1*

If the Word is God and God is Omnipotent, that means God's Word is all-powerful. Therefore, every genuine encounter with the Word empowers people to do the impossible.

Apostle Paul said: ***For I am not ashamed of the gospel of Christ: for it is the power of God unto salvation to every one that believeth; to the Jew first, and also to the Greek*** (Romans 1:16).

It is also written: ***...as many as received him, to them gave he power to become the sons of God, even to them that believe on his name:*** (John 1:12).

When we receive the Word, we are empowered by it to manifest our true sonship. That is, every Word we receive empowers us to become what it says. Every revelation we encounter empowers us for manifestation.

God's Word is as omnipotent as He is, because in the beginning was the Word and the Word was with God and the Word was God. Therefore, whatever God is, that is what His Word is. God's Word can, therefore, be defined as omnipotent because it is all-powerful, invincible and undefeatable in any conflict. God's Word reigns supreme.

For instance, we understand that God rules by the power of His Word forever. The Bible says:

> ***The Lord said unto my Lord, Sit thou at my right hand, until I make thine enemies thy footstool. The Lord shall send the rod of thy strength out of Zion: rule thou in the midst of thine enemies. Thy people shall be willing in the day of thy power, in the beauties of holiness from the womb of the morning: thou hast the dew of thy youth.***
>
> *Psalm 110:1-3*

Most of our battles, if not all, are against the powers of darkness and until we allow the Word to rule our hearts, we remain in darkness. It is written:

> ***For we wrestle not against flesh and blood, but against principalities, against powers, against the rulers of the darkness of this world, against spiritual wickedness in high places.***
>
> *Ephesians 6:12*

The wickedness of the enemy is always in the realm of darkness and what it takes to deal with that is light, which has rule over darkness any day, anytime and anywhere. When I refer to light, I mean the light of the Word.

And the light shineth in darkness; and the darkness comprehended it not.

That was the true Light, which lighteth every man that cometh into the world.

John 1:5, 9

Hence, every genuine encounter with the Word lightens us up and turns us to spiritual "illuminants". This empowers us to dominate all the powers of darkness around us.

In 1996, a woman who lived in Port Harcourt (a city in Nigeria) and was an evangelist was suffering from insomnia. She couldn't sleep because some evil forces attacked her at night. When she complained to me, I told her that I would give her three tablets that would make her sleep like a baby from that time. I gave her three scriptures that entitled her to sound sleep.

When the demon came that night, she rose with one of the scriptures and the demon was suspended in the air. That gave her confidence. She shut another arrow of the Word and it fled forever. After that, Jesus conquered that spirit of insomnia and she began to sleep normally.

God's Word lightens us and that light empowers us to conquer the forces of darkness. It is this darkness that is responsible for the stagnation of God's children. Every true encounter with the Word empowers us to overcome the forces of darkness.

By an encounter with the light of the Word, we dispel and disarm all the forces of darkness because we are empowered for conquest. Therefore, at all realms, God's Word empowers us to live a more than conqueror's life.

Our only guarantee for triumph in every conflict with darkness is light, because we naturally believe what we see and what we believe, we are supernaturally empowered to become. Nobody ever doubts what he sees, and what light does is to help us see what God is saying. Thus, light brings us into realms of spiritual understanding which makes our faith become automatic and by that, conquest becomes a walkover.

The Healing Power of the Word

God's Word carries His nature, which is immune to sicknesses and diseases. When we receive and believe the Word, we buy into divine nature that establishes our dominion over every assault on our bodies.

The Centurion said to Jesus: ***...but speak the word only, and my servant shall be healed*** (Matthew 8:8).

It is also written: ***My son, attend to my words; incline thine ear unto my sayings. Let them not depart from thine eyes; keep them in the midst of thine heart. For they are life unto those that find them, and health to***

all their flesh (Proverbs 4:20-22).

When we receive the Word and believe it, divine health is imparted into us. That is, we dominate every assault on our body and soul, thereby commanding dominion over sicknesses and diseases. Every time God's Word goes forth, God's healing power goes forth. That is why we are told that Jesus, the living Word, went about doing good and healing all that were oppressed of the devil.

> ***And it came to pass on a certain day, as he was teaching, that there were Pharisees and doctors of the law sitting by, which were come out of every town of Galilee, and Judaea, and Jerusalem: and the power of the Lord was present to heal them.***
>
> *Luke 5:17*

All our inheritances in Christ are locked up in the Scriptures and healing is one of our redemptive heritages in Christ. He took our infirmities and bore our sicknesses. No doubt, therefore, God's Word is the principal balm in Gilead because it can heal any sickness and disease. When we receive the Word concerning our inheritance of divine health, the healing power of God is released to make us whole (Luke 6:17-19).

> ***And now, brethren, I commend you to God, and to the word of his grace, which is able to build you up, and to give you an inheritance among all them which***

are sanctified.

Acts 20:32

Therefore, when we receive and believe God's Word, His healing power flows into our lives. There is a dynamic healing force in the Word of God, which has the capacity to reverse any situation at any time, if we let Him do it (Job 33:21-25).

Deliverance in the Word

We understand from the Scriptures that the light of the Word of God is irresistible to the powers of darkness. There is deliverance power in the Word and its light empowers us for dominion over the powers of darkness.

We must recognise that we are contending with invisible forces on a daily basis, but revelation of the Word is our guarantee for victory.

Darkness is the highest realm that the enemy operates in to perform his wicked works. However, when we put on the armour of light, we disarm him as if nothing existed before. Thus, walking in the light empowers us to always triumph over darkness.

We must understand that it is the savour of revelation, that is, the mysteries in the Word of God, that keeps us triumphing. No wonder the devil continues to resist our access to the light of the gospel. Our victory in this conflict is the revelation of the truth (Psalm 91:5-10).

As it is written: ***And ye shall know the truth, and the truth shall make you free*** (John 8:32).

When there is light in us, we cannot stumble because darkness flees at our instance; and the entrance of God's Word gives light.

> ***The entrance of thy words giveth light; it giveth understanding unto the simple.***
>
> *Psalm 119:130*

Years ago, I got so enraged by one little daughter in the family who claimed to be behind the torture and torment of her parents. I already knew my authority over the powers of darkness, so I wanted us to have a playing field. One night, I, in the company of one of my associates, drove her to the bush.

When we got there, I ordered her to do anything I told her to do. When I asked her why the devil could not come to help her, she said: "As long as you are here, he cannot come."

If we can see that we have been repositioned, we will stop being tormented.

It is one thing to receive the Word and another to believe it. A combination of the two is what empowers us for dominion.

> ***But as many as received him, to them gave he power to become the sons of God, even to them that believe***

on his name:

John 1:12

The word "even" means we believing equally whatever we have received, then we are empowered to manifest as sons of God. Most times, what we hear is powerless until we believe it; and what we receive is helpless until we believe it. It is a combination of receiving and believing that empowers our full-scale manifestation. Thus, it is not enough to receive the Word; we must go a little further to believe the Word and then, we dominate our circumstances.

TWO

DISCOVERING OUR SPIRITUAL IDENTITY

...and hast redeemed us to God by thy blood out of every kindred, and tongue, and people, and nation; And hast made us unto our God kings and priests: and we shall reign on the earth.

Revelation 5:9-10

Understanding our identity in Christ has been a major challenge among believers. Most of the time, Christians don't really understand who they are and what they carry. That is why the devil can molest their destinies, because they lack an understanding of what they have by redemption.

According to Hosea 4:6, we understand that believers

are destroyed for lack of knowledge. This knowledge can be likened to their inability to see who they are according to the Scriptures.

A revelation of our spiritual identity is our greatest asset in the journey of life. That is what positions us for dominion in the adventures of life.

It is written concerning Jesus: ***Then said they unto him, Who art thou? And Jesus saith unto them, Even the same that I said unto you from the beginning*** (John 8:25).

Jesus had an understanding of His identity, and that was the reason for His mighty exploits. For instance, anytime law enforcement agents are to search you, they tell you to "Identify yourself". This is because our identity is our strength, security and authority. Without our identity, we can be termed as "lost" and without recognition.

However, our understanding of the worth of our destiny is the only way not to sell off our birthright like Esau did. He sold his birthright for a morsel of meat and wept bitterly afterwards, but it was too late. We must understand that we cannot get our desired turnaround without an understanding of who we are, what we have and what qualifies us for that experience.

I heard a story that Kenneth E. Hagin told many years ago. He said that a lion cub was captured and it grew among sheep; as a result, it lost its identity as a lion. It ate with the sheep, behaved and grew up like them. Every time they went to the stream to drink water and they sighted a lion on the other side, each one took to its heels, including the "lion-sheep".

One day, when the "lion-sheep" saw its reflection on the surface of the water, it dawned on it that it resembled the animal they usually ran away from and that encounter changed its mentality. The next time they went to the stream and saw a lion, all the sheep took to their heels except the "lion-sheep". It wagged its tail, crossed to the other side and when the other lions met it, they welcomed it back to the family.

Most of the time, the reason we lose our identity is because, we live in the natural realm. We must understand that we have our supernatural identity and we need to discover that identity from the Scriptures because that is where our actual picture is found.

Knowing our spiritual identity begins with the discovery of our root in Christ. This entails understanding who we are, who lives in us, what we have, and where we stand in Christ. When we have an understanding of these points, we qualify for outstanding results. As we obtain such results, we begin to command turnarounds in all areas of life.

In discovering our identity, we must note that it can

only be seen in the Word of God. God's Word is loaded with wonders and only those who see those wonders can experience them. One principal wonder that the Word carries is to unveil our identity. Until we are conscious of our identity in Christ, we cannot gain command to operate on earth. Therefore, it is when we receive the Word that the wonders in it begin to manifest in our lives.

Identifying ourselves in the Word is our place of command. Everyone who would make any serious impact in life must discover his identity in Christ. For instance, the reason I say some dangerous things is because of the consciousness of my identity. You don't have to mind what people say about you. Apostle Paul said, "We cannot but speak the things which we have seen and heard" (Acts 4:20).

One day, through the powerful ministry of Smith Wigglesworth, I saw that I am seated with Christ in heavenly places, far above; and that gave me authority over the devil and his agents. I cannot be tormented by any trick of the devil, because I have an understanding of who I am in Christ.

In 1979, I concluded a teaching in a secondary school, and before the altar call for salvation, I asked, "How many of you are witches here? Stand up." I saw a large crowd in response to that call; so, I had to make sure they knew what I was talking about. When eventually

I was sure that they understood me, I called one of them and asked, "What do you do with the devil?"

She said, "When we are thirsty for blood, we go to the highway and cause vehicles to somersault, so we can suck the blood of the victims." Then with full authority I asked, "What of when people like us are coming?" She replied, "When we sense a higher power, we clear off the highway."

This validates the statement made by an armed robber who testified of how he came with his gang to rob in one of our services. According to him, when they came in, they saw flames of fire on everyone's head and as a result, they could not operate. Therefore, we must understand that we are not "ordinary" and that means we are not permitted to be molested by the devil and his agents. I want you to believe that picture of your worth from the Scriptures because what you discover from the Scriptures will change your mentality forever!

Who art Thou?

Jesus knew who He was and that was the greatest challenge of the devil. When we discover our true identity, we dominate the circumstances of life. On several occasions, the devil moved people to attempt to stone Jesus and it was all because of the consciousness of His identity (John 5:17-18, 8:58-59).

It is written: ***Jesus answered them, Is it not written in your law, I said, Ye are gods? If he called them gods, unto whom the word of God came, and the Scripture cannot be broken; Say ye of him, whom the Father hath sanctified, and sent into the world, Thou blasphemest; because I said, I am the Son of God? If I do not the works of my Father, believe me not. But if I do, though ye believe not me, believe the works: that ye may know, and believe, that the Father is in me, and I in him. Therefore they sought again to take him: but he escaped out of their hand*** (John 10:34-39).

The revelation of our identity is our greatest asset, because it positions us for dominion in the adventures of life. We must recognise that as believers, our case is different!

For instance, the Bible says: ***But ye are a chosen generation, a royal priesthood, an holy nation, a peculiar people; that ye should shew forth the praises of him who hath called you out of darkness into his marvellous light*** (1 Peter 2:9).

We are chosen to live marvellous lives, because in the Scriptures, light equals life. In Him was life and the life was the light of men (John 1:4). By redemption, we are ordained to live marvellous lives – a life to be wondered at. That is the God kind of life! When we are saved, our human life is exchanged for divine life.

The Word is a divine mirror in which we discover

our personalities. That is, the Word of God paints the picture of our person, and that is the platform for our dominion and authority. The hotter our revelation, the brighter we will shine. When we understand our identity in redemption, we secure our glorious destiny in a grand style. That is the baseline for our faith and strength; recognising and operating in the consciousness of who we are.

What are our Peculiarities?

The child of a man possesses human life; the kid of a goat possesses goat's life, and the offspring of a fish, possesses fish life. Therefore, every child of God possesses the life of God.

Salvation is a translation from humanity to divinity. We possess the life of God, so we can live like Him. Eternal life is the God kind of life, which we encounter through salvation. Thus, we can't say as humans, "What can I do under this circumstance?" That means we are ignorant. When we are saved, we are not ordinary beings; we are God-beings in human clothing, and God always knows what to do in any circumstance.

It is written: ***But as many as received him, to them gave he power to become the sons of God, even to them that believe on his name:*** (John 1:12)

I don't want you to just consent to that statement, I

want you to see it, because until you are convinced that you have divine life in place of human life, you cannot experience it.

He said: ***Behold, what manner of love the Father hath bestowed upon us, that we should be called the sons of God: therefore the world knoweth us not, because it knew him not. Beloved, now are we the sons of God, and it doth not yet appear what we shall be: but we know that, when he shall appear, we shall be like him; for we shall see him as he is*** (1 John 3:1-2).

We must understand that everyone who is born again is a child of God that possesses the God kind of life; and that life is immune to sicknesses, pains, setbacks, failures and every evil. Before the fall of man, there was no pain, ache, sickness or disease. Adam physically possessed the life of God; he had no fear, and so, there was no torment.

That was man at the beginning before the fall; and Jesus came to restore what was lost in the first Adam. That means, redemption gives us our heritage in God. Therefore, we can't partake of the hereditary diseases in our natural family, because we don't belong there anymore. What affects them must not affect us, because we don't belong to the same lineage again; we now belong to God's lineage. That translation should form our mentality.

It is written: ***Therefore if any man be in Christ, he is a new creature: old things are passed away; behold, all things are become new*** (2 Corinthians 5:17).

It is also written: ***The Spirit itself beareth witness with our spirit, that we are the children of God: And if children, then heirs; heirs of God, and joint-heirs with Christ; if so be that we suffer with him, that we may be also glorified together*** (Romans 8:16-17).

Also, Jesus is the Lion of the tribe of Judah and that is the winning tribe among the tribes of Israel. He said, ***Judah is a lion's whelp: my son,...who shall rouse him up?*** (Genesis 49:9). Thus, redemption makes us winning sons. No matter the heat of the battle, victory is determined in our favour. We can't be brothers of a lion, except we are lions (Revelation 5:5).

The lion is ordained to prevail, no matter the heat of the battle. No matter the gang up from hell, you are ordained for victory. Therefore, from today, the last battle you lost is the last you will ever lose!

If Jesus called us brethren and He is the Lion of the tribe of Judah, then we are lions. As a result, we are bound to always prevail. It is that picture of the lion in me that gives me the winning mentality in every battle; because the lion is strongest among beasts and turns not away for any. Lions are never known with fear, they only set fear in others; the consciousness of the lion in us will make us fearless.

It is written: ***Now thanks be unto God, which always causeth us to triumph in Christ, and maketh manifest the savour of his knowledge by us in every place*** (2 Corinthians 2:14).

Furthermore, we discover from the Scriptures that redemption has repositioned us above all principalities and powers; so, we are not just saved and left at the mercy of the devil.

It is written: ***Who hath delivered us from the power of darkness, and hath translated us into the kingdom of his dear Son*** (Colossians 1:13).

We no longer live in the devil's domain; we are far above. As great as the American nation is, no American law enforcement agent can arrest you in Nigeria, because you are off their territory. We need the consciousness that salvation has translated us from the realm where principalities and powers dominate and torment. We have left their kingdom; hence, their constitution is no longer binding on us. Also, their law enforcement agents cannot arrest or harass us because Christ has raised us together with Him.

> ***Even when we were dead in sins, hath quickened us together with Christ, (by grace ye are saved;) And hath raised us up together, and made us sit together in heavenly places in Christ Jesus:***
>
> *Ephesians 2:5-6*

By redemption, we have become heavenly citizens; we are only on assignment on the earth. Therefore, whatever does not obtain in heaven is illegal in our lives!

We must understand, therefore, that to command dominion on the earth, we need a heavenly mentality. I have had that mentality since 1979 and no one can get me off it forever! There is no force under heaven that can rouse fear in me; I can only stir up fear in them. This is because, I am not in their realm; I left there a long time ago by revelation.

It is written: ***Which he wrought in Christ, when he raised him from the dead, and set him at his own right hand in the heavenly places, Far above all principality, and power, and might, and dominion, and every name that is named, not only in this world, but also in that which is to come*** (Ephesians 1:20-21).

Can you imagine a dog chasing a lion, because it is a German dog? The devil is roaring like a lion but that does not make him a lion; he is only a barking dog. There is only one Lion in the Scripture; His name is Jesus, the Lion of the tribe of Judah! Therefore, we must not allow any circumstance to outweigh us, because we are seated far above that realm of failure, worries and shame.

Also, among our peculiarities by redemption is that

we are translated to be signs and wonders. That is, to live in the realm of the supernatural (John 3:8). Hence, every child of God is a man and a woman to be wondered at, because our steps should provoke the exclamation, "Wow!" from every quarter.

The consciousness of the supernatural is the guarantee for breakthroughs in the journey of life. Walking in the supernatural is the root to our all-round success and it is what distinguishes the Christian faith from all other faiths. Therefore, operating by the Word is operating in signs and wonders.

God has spoken so many things to you, but you don't have the capacity to receive them because you are operating in the natural realm. However, when you are born again, you are like the wind, no one can tell where you are coming from or where you are headed. Jesus said: ***...so is everyone that is born of the spirit*** (John 3:8).

Moreover, redemption engraces us with the mind of Christ, which is above every intellectual capacity and it puts us ahead of all. It is written: ***For who hath known the mind of the Lord, that he may instruct him? But we have the mind of Christ*** (1 Corinthians 2:16).

What is that Mind Worth?

The mind of Christ is the epitome of soundness,

wholesomeness and excellence. From the moment we become born again, our minds no longer operate in the natural realm. We begin to think at the level of divinity, where we have been translated to. This is why we need to develop our minds in the Word to know our worth.

Our natural minds are exchanged for His divine mind, so we can operate at the same frequency, generating the same order of results. Operating with the mind of Christ is the ultimate of creativity. There will be a time in the body of Christ, when we will operate in a wave of divine intuition, because the reality of the mind of Christ is returning to the church.

There is a divine deposit inside us that needs to be released. The mind we have now is the same mind that created the universe and everything we see today. Thus, that mind can turn any situation around, but we only need to believe it.

The Bible says, ***For whatsoever is born of God overcometh the world, and this is the victory that overcometh the world, even our faith*** (I John 5:4). That means, what we believe about ourselves from the Scriptures is what makes us overcomers. If we understand this picture, then we are more than conquerors. That means, the contender can't wait for us to arrive in the ring.

People pride themselves in who they know and the family they come from; but we are from the family of God and we have Jesus Christ as our brother. Therefore, no gate can be shut against us!

Friend, a lot has been deposited inside us that we cannot afford to remain the way we are or be tormented by the devil. We need to settle down with the Word, so we can gain command of circumstances of life. Your turnaround has finally come!

Therefore, to access all that Christ died for on our behalf, we need a mind-transplant. This implies trading our natural minds with that of divinity. We are to renew our minds through encounters with the Word. The Bible says:

> ***And be not conformed to this world: but be ye transformed by the renewing of your mind, that ye may prove what is that good, and acceptable, and perfect, will of God.***
>
> *Romans 12:2*

However, it is important to note that we cannot fly higher than the mentality we possess. This is because it is what we can see that we are empowered to become, thereby commanding unending turnarounds (John 1:12). Henceforth, this shall be your testimony in Jesus' name!

THREE

GAINING COMMAND

For I will give you a mouth and wisdom, which all your adversaries shall not be able to gainsay nor resist.

Luke 21:15

Every child of God has a great destiny in Christ. We are not redeemed to be pitied, but to be envied by the world. The devil raises several oppositions to deny us access to our glorious destinies in Christ; hence, as great as our destinies are, so are the oppositions against them. That is why we need to gain command over any opposition that may want to harass our destinies or confront our turnarounds.

When Moses, a man of great destiny, was born, Pharaoh went after all the Hebrew male infants and slaughtered them, in search of him. Also, when Christ the Messiah came, Herod rose after the order of Pharaoh and he killed every male infant, in search of Jesus the Messiah. This shows how the enemy is so determined to stop God's glorious plans for our lives (Exodus 1:22, 2:1-10; Matthew 2:1-16).

The only way to deal with this adversary is to take command of the outcome of our lives. We must understand that God does not only want us to have spiritual turnarounds; but also to be physically, mentally, psychologically, financially and emotionally sound. Therefore, we must know how to deal with the adversary or our colourful destinies may remain shut.

It is not the conflict that determines the victory; but we determine our victory in any conflict of life, because we shall have whatsoever we say. The Word will always deliver, but not without us using it to gain command over every issue.

We need to understand that we cannot gain or give out command without authority. The word "command" connotes exercise of authority, and except we walk in the steps of giants, we cannot command results after their order.

The Centurion met Jesus and said, ***...speak the word only, and my servant shall be healed. For I am a man under authority, having soldiers under me: and I say to this man, Go, and he goeth; and to another, Come, and he cometh; and to my servant, Do this and he doeth it. And Jesus said unto the centurion, Go thy***

way; and as thou hast believed, so be it done unto thee. And his servant was healed in the selfsame hour (Matthew 8:8-9, 13).

That is a turnaround command! We must be conscious of the source of our authority before we can be in command.

In the above scripture, there was an instant turnaround in operation and that came from a source of authority. We must understand that we have authority, but we cannot exercise it without being under the superior authority of the One that gives all things. That means, as believers, we have authority in Christ, but to command authority we must subject and submit ourselves to the source, which is God.

Also, as heirs of the Kingdom of God, we are redeemed to be kings and to reign on the earth. Everyone that is born again, out of every kindred, every tongue and every people is ordained to rule. If we are redeemed as kings, then we are kings under the King of kings (Revelation 5:9-10).

As it is written: His name shall be called ***...KING OF KINGS, AND LORD OF LORDS*** (Revelation 19:16).

Therefore, to enforce or command our turnaround experience, we must:

Exercise Authority

Authority cannot be acquired or attained; it can only

be conferred. In Matthew 21:23, the Jews questioned the authority of Jesus saying: ***...By what authority doest thou these things? And who gave thee this authority?***

Authority is exercised by the word coming from the source of the authority.

He said: ***Who is he that saith, and it cometh to pass, when the Lord commandeth it not?*** (Lamentations 3:37).

Jesus gave His disciples power and authority over all devils and to cure all diseases. He gave them power, but that power became effectual by the authority He conferred on them.

> ***For as the Father hath life in himself; so hath he given to the Son to have life in himself; And hath given him authority to execute judgment also, because he is the Son of man.***
>
> *John 5:26-27*

Even Jesus was not in command by power; He was in command by the authority conferred on Him.

We command a turnaround by recognising the level of authority placed in us. One may crave, thirst and fast for power, but authority is only conferred. We cannot fast or pray for it; it can only be received by the sent word. The authority that gives us command over all circumstances and situations can only be conferred on us by the Holy Ghost.

It is impossible to operate in the realm of the supernatural without being empowered by the Holy Ghost to take charge. This is why every child of God must be baptised in the Holy Ghost with the evidence of speaking in tongues, in order to walk in the supernatural.

Possess a True Knowledge of our Identity

As emphasised in the previous chapter, a discovery of our actual identity in Christ empowers us to exercise authority. We need to know who we are, or we will never gain command. Our level of authority is a function of our depth of understanding about our position in Christ.

New birth is not a religious experience; it is a spiritual transformation into divinity. It is the importation of divine nature into the human vessel. It is not enough to be born again, we must be conscious of the worth of our salvation. This is what distinguishes us from others who claim to be believers.

As believers, we must seek to have access to the mysteries of God's Word, because the clarity of our picture from the Word determines our clarity of command in the supernatural. If we can see our worth through the Scriptures and activate ourselves into the flow from the Word, we will begin to command authority for definite turnarounds.

The Word is a catalyst for our manifestation. Abraham

operated by the Word of the Lord consistently, and God wants us blessed after the order of Abraham. This is confirmed in several scriptures. He wants us to experience unhindered turnarounds in our journey. That is God's agenda!

> ***...If ye were Abraham's children, ye would do the works of Abraham.***
>
> *John 8:39*

Therefore, if we must command results after the order of Abraham, we must have access to the Word from the Lord concerning our challenges. Nothing delivers like our faith, and faith is drawn from the revelation of the Word and the spiritual understanding of it concerning our situations.

God said, ***Look unto Abraham your father, and unto Sarah that bare you: for I called him alone, and blessed him, and increased him*** (Isaiah 51:2).

That is, we need to position ourselves like Abraham, ensure that we have access to the Word from the Lord like him and we will have Abraham's kind of results.

Know the Source of Command

Knowing the source of our command helps to boost our confidence. Jesus is always on key and ever in control. He said, "As I hear," meaning He worked as directed by the Father. Jesus said in John 5:26-27: ***For as the Father hath life in himself; so hath he given to***

the Son to have life in himself; And hath given him authority...

In verse 30, He talked about the source of His authority. He said, "I can of mine own self do nothing: as I hear, I judge: and my judgment is just..."

Even though by redemption, we are positioned to take charge, it takes a word from the Lord to gain command. "As I hear", not "as I read", or "as they said." As I hear from the Father, so I determine and decide what happens and I am always in charge.

Therefore, our source of command is a word from the Lord, which will terminate every struggle of life and empower us to take charge of our situations. Every word from God brings about a definite turnaround, provided we are sure enough to believe the word and act on it.

Engage the Holy Spirit

He is the Carrier, Communicator and Transmitter of the power of God. He is the power from on high and whatever is from above is above all. Therefore, when confronted with any issue of concern, we can always engage the invincible force of the Holy Spirit.

We must understand that God's mighty power is domicile in the Holy Spirit and so, He is important to our gaining command over every challenge that confronts us. Therefore, nothing is permitted to resist our progress, success, accomplishments, exploits or breakthroughs, when the Holy Spirit is at work.

> ***Behold, I give unto you power to tread on serpents and scorpions, and over all the power of the enemy: and nothing shall by any means hurt you.***
>
> *Luke 10:19*

The Holy Ghost is the person behind the mystery of the Word that gives us mastery. He is called the Teacher! He teaches and gives us understanding of every scripture that makes us capture our future in the Scriptures, because He will remind us of our sent Word so we can war with it.

> ***But the Comforter, which is the Holy Ghost, whom the Father will send in my name, he shall teach you all things, and bring all things to your remembrance, whatsoever I have said unto you.***
>
> *John 14:26*

The Holy Ghost is the custodian of the mysteries of the Kingdom of God. Anybody can access the stories, because they are found on familiar grounds, but the mysteries are the direct operation of the Holy Ghost. He teaches the mysteries by instructing our spirit.

> ***I have yet many things to say unto you, but ye cannot bear them now. Howbeit when he, the Spirit of truth, is come, he will guide you into all truth: for he shall not speak of himself; but whatsoever he shall hear, that shall he speak: and he will shew you things to come.***
>
> *John 16:12-13*

From that scripture, the Holy Ghost is known as the Spirit of truth. When going through any difficult situation, we can inquire from Him. When He is involved in our cases, He grants us access to the truth and every time we know the truth, we are set free. Nonetheless, we must understand that the Holy Ghost cannot teach us how to gain command until our spirit is connected to Him.

Our gaining command over every issue we are confronted with requires access to rhema—revelations from God via His Word. Rhema is powerful and it can only be received with the help of the Holy Ghost. The Holy Spirit has been given to us to minister and to show us things to come. Therefore, we must trust Him to reveal what our future holds. We must get to the point where we operate solely by His guidance. As we advance in the Holy Spirit, our level of command in the supernatural advances.

Engage the Word

The Word, which is the main emphasis in this book, is the major medium through which we gain command. The voice of the Lord is behind every statement of the Scriptures and with the power in the Word, we dominate every circumstance of life.

> ***Seek ye out of the book of the Lord, and read: no one of these shall fail, none shall want her mate,***

> ***for my mouth it has commanded it, and my spirit it has gathered it.***
>
> *Isaiah 34:16*

The Holy Ghost turns the written Word to a voice. When the Word fills our hearts and rules our minds, it manifests naturally through the words we speak. Behind every scripture is the voice of His Majesty; when it rules our spirit, we gain command automatically.

It is written, "Arise, shine; for thy light is come..." (Isaiah 60:1). The Word is that light and its effect empowers us to outshine those around us, to the extent that kings begin to come to the brightness of our light, which brings about our rising. This is because revelation has the power to supernaturally change the story of a man (Isaiah 60:3, 8, 22).

Every true encounter with the Word gives us command over the issues that confront us and when we have command over such issues, we gain mastery over them.

We must understand that God's Word is pregnant with wonders and that is why all miracles, deliverances, breakthroughs, signs and wonders are direct confirmations of the Word (Mark 16:20).

FOUR

ACCESSING THE WORD

Thy words were found, and I did eat them; and thy word was unto me the joy and rejoicing of mine heart: for I am called by thy name, O Lord God of hosts.

Jeremiah 15:16

How do we have access to our own stone of victory and armour of light? How do we stand strong in the day of battle? These are questions to be answered in this chapter. We need to have an understanding of how to get the right word to tackle our situations, because a particular key cannot open every door. The Word is the key to our turnaround, and we need the right key to experience that turnaround.

As it is written: ***And now, brethren, I commend you to God, and to the word of his grace, which is able to build you up, and to give you an inheritance among***

all them which are sanctified (Acts 20:32).

It is the Word that gives us command and the Word is the light that shatters every dark area of our lives. Hence, we have an inheritance in God's Word which gives us access to that turnaround we desire.

The Word is loaded; it is the answer to every question, the solution to every problem and the way out of every predicament. God's Word is everything to man. When God's Word is rejected, the individual becomes a victim of life, because the only solution to darkness is light. Therefore, when we turn our backs on light, we become victims of darkness and the Word is the only true light. There are various kinds of light but the true light that illuminates every man that comes into the world is God's Word (John 1:1-12).

That makes the Word the guarantee for our long desired success and prosperity. It is written: ***This book of the law shall not depart out of thy mouth; but thou shalt meditate therein day and night, that thou mayest observe to do according to all that is written therein: for then thou shalt make thy way prosperous, and then thou shalt have good success*** (Joshua 1:8).

Also, referring to our colourful destiny, the Bible says:

> ***And it shall come to pass, if thou shalt hearken diligently unto the voice of the LORD thy God, to observe and to do all his commandments which I***

command thee this day, that the LORD thy God will set thee on high above all nations of the earth:

And all these blessings shall come on thee, and overtake thee, if thou shalt hearken unto the voice of the LORD thy God.

Blessed shalt thou be in the city, and blessed shalt thou be in the field.

Deuteronomy 28:1-3

This proves that the Bible, the voice of His majesty, is the answer-book of life. It carries God's master plan for His people because it tells us where we are headed in destiny and how to get there. However, there is a platform we must attain, to be able to access the revelation of the truth. In Revelation 4:1, God said: "...Come up hither, and I will shew thee things which must be hereafter." We cannot see it out there on the floor; that is why He said, "Come up!" Many hear what God is saying, but very few see it. If we want to see what God is saying, we need to come up to His level.

How, then, can we Access the Revelation of the Truth?

Be Born Again

We understand that the Bible is made up of mysteries and these mysteries are God's secrets behind every biblical story. However, it is the unveiling of these secrets and their application that gives us the turnarounds we desire.

To an ordinary man, the Scripture is made up of stories. Therefore, until we are redeemed, we cannot access the mysteries therein. The stories are made up of letters, while the mysteries are made up of Spirit and life. Without the impartation of the life in the Word, we can only access the stories of the Word; we cannot access the wonders in it.

Jesus said: ***...Unto you it is given to know the mystery of the kingdom of God: but unto them that are without, all these things are done in parables*** (Mark 4:11).

Hence, we need to spiritually align by being born again, so we can access the Spirit virtue in the Word. Our destinies are limited by our access to the Word and the Bible states that except we are born-again we cannot see or gain access to the truth in the Word. Thus, by salvation, which entails accepting Jesus in our lives, we gain access to the treasures in the Word for our turnarounds.

Be Spiritual

It is very interesting to know that even though God's Word is the heritage of the redeemed, it is only accessible by spirituality. As long as we are carnal, we cannot access light from heaven.

This is the greatest challenge of the church today. There are men who are filled with the Spirit, but only few truly walk in the Spirit. They do not allow themselves to be used by the Holy Spirit, even when they are filled.

It is written: ***I was in the spirit on the Lord's Day, and heard behind me a great voice, as of a trumpet*** (Revelation 1:10).

The above scripture clearly emphasises that we must be in the Spirit to hear what God is saying to us per time. That means our spirit-man needs to be actively alive, if we must engage heaven and hear God's voice. This is because the Words of God are spiritual stones and arrows needed to turn around every situation of our lives.

As it is also written: ***Which things also we speak, not in the words which man's wisdom teacheth, but which the Holy Ghost teacheth; comparing spiritual things with spiritual. But the natural man receiveth not the things of the Spirit of God: for they are foolishness unto him: neither can he know them, because they are spiritually discerned*** (1 Corinthians 2:13-14).

When we are spiritual, we gain free access to the things of God because the Holy Spirit, Who is the custodian of divine secrets, can only speak with our spirit. Thus, it is only the spiritual that can hear Him; and we need His direction to harass every situation that confronts our turnarounds.

Being spiritual simply means, we exalt the things that are written in the Scriptures, higher than what nature tells us. We must understand that carnality will always rob a man of his dignity and true value! The Bible says: ***For to be carnally minded is death; but to be spiritually minded is life and peace*** (Romans 8:6).

Carnality has no place in commanding a turnaround. Most of the time, we approach things carnally, that is why we don't get positive results. There is a need, therefore, to have a change of approach, so our reproach can be rolled off.

Our approach to God's Word must be spiritually empowered by taking His Word as the word of life. We must see it as a daily necessity for living. Those who take God's Word as nutrients, naturally gain command of the issues of life, because they are ever strong. The devil cannot take advantage of them because they are weighty.

As we know, life's battles are essentially spiritual, because they are fought in the spiritual realm. As such, a natural man can never gain mastery over supernatural situations. The Bible says that the devil is the enemy and we cannot see him; therefore, we cannot handle him with physical weapons.

For the weapons of our warfare are not carnal, but mighty through God to the pulling down of strong holds (2 Corinthians 10:4).

Though we live in this world, we are not of this world. We are not like those outside the fold; there is something peculiar, uncommon and unusual about us. However, we must remain spiritual, to keep flowing in unusual dimensions.

Many people are "lightweight" and the devil defeats them on any minor issue. When we take a daily dose of God's Word in season, out of season, morning and night, we would approach every issue of our lives with His Word. The Word becomes our lifestyle because, in Him, we live, move and have our being.

It is written: ***Turn you at my reproof: behold, I will pour out my spirit unto you, I will make known my words unto you*** (Proverbs 1:23).

Also, we must make conscious effort to approach God's Word as life-nutrient, not only as bullets of attack. When we take God's Word as life-nutrient, we are naturally vaccinated!

In Luke 10:42, Jesus said: ***But one thing is needful***... Spirituality is our principal need to access our Word of command. When that Word comes, our command becomes unquestionable. There is need for us to press in order to obtain a prize. Only pressers end up as prizewinners. We need to press into the Word, and answer specific questions that would lead to our turnarounds.

As it is written: ***...the kingdom of God is preached, and every man presseth into it*** (Luke 16:16).

Spirituality will always qualify us for an understanding of the Word. It takes spiritual men to access the truths in the Scripture and if we are not spiritual, we disqualify ourselves from accessing the mysteries of the Kingdom; and it is by these mysteries that we gain masteries over the issues of life.

Be Filled with the Holy Spirit

We need the baptism of the Holy Spirit to break the limit off our access to the Word; otherwise, we are limited. The Holy Spirit enhances our access to the Word and brings us into realms of unlimited depth in the things of God, for He teaches us all things and without Him, we know nothing.

Jesus said to His disciples, "I have many things to say unto you, but ye cannot bear them now. Howbeit when he, the Spirit of truth, is come, He will guide you into all truth..." (John 16:12). And the Holy Spirit is the Spirit of truth.

As it is written: ***But the Comforter, which is the Holy Ghost, whom the Father will send in my name, he shall***

teach you all things, and bring all things to your remembrance, whatsoever I have said unto you (John 14:26).

The Holy Spirit is real! When Peter exploded in revelation on the day of Pentecost, there was no way to access that realm except by the Holy Spirit. He was a professor in ministry, without opening any notebook.

But God hath revealed them unto us by his Spirit: for the Spirit searcheth all things, yea, the deep things of God (1 Corinthians 2:10).

Every believer is limited in access without the Holy Spirit. The anointing of the Holy Spirit is the vital factor to gaining access to the truth. Many read the Bible, but are not connected to the mysteries because the things that make for our turnaround are not contained on the shallow surface, but in the deep, and only the Holy Spirit can take us to that depth.

We Must Thirst for the Word

> ***Ho, every one that thirsteth, come ye to the waters, and he that hath no money; come ye, buy, and eat; yea, come, buy wine and milk without money and without price.***
>
> *Isaiah 55:1*

There is a price to pay to gain access to our own word of command. It is a thirst price. In Agricultural Science, we understand that it is easy for sandy soil to get water because it is porous, but clay soil is thick; water cannot easily flow into it. We need to create a sandy situation around our hearts and that is where being thirsty comes in. There is always a need to create a thirst by which God's Word moves us without restriction.

As it is written: ***And he said unto me, it is done. I am Alpha and Omega, the beginning and the end. I will give unto him that is athirst of the fountain of the water of life freely*** (Revelation 21:6).

It takes a thirst to access the Word for our turnaround encounter. That is why the Bible says: ***Come, all you who are thirsty, come to the waters...*** (Isaiah 55:1 NIV).

The thirstier we are, the freer God gives us His Word. Our degree of access to God's Word is directly proportional to our degree of thirst. Therefore, when a thirsty person meets with a giving God, it produces a supernatural turnaround and an encounter with destiny. Our turning points depend on our degree of thirst. Hence, we need to press with a thirst!

Connect to the Ministry of Teaching Priests

God has always made available to the church, apostles, prophets, evangelists, pastors and teachers to help provoke us through the authorship of anointed, life-changing, destiny-moulding books that are packaged to help us understand how best to put the Word of God to work.

The ministry of the teaching priest is vital to our quest for light (the Word) that leads to our turnarounds. These teaching priests are endowed with divine access to unusual light, which grants us access to our own light.

Concerning Israel, the Bible records: ***Now for a long season Israel hath been without the true God, and without a teaching priest and without law. But when they in their trouble did turn unto the LORD God of Israel, and sought him, he was found of them. And when Asa heard these words, and the prophecy of Oded the prophet, he took courage, and put away the abominable idols out of all the land of Judah and Benjamin, and out of the cities which he had taken from mount Ephraim, and renewed the altar of the LORD, that was before the porch of the LORD*** (2 Chronicles 15:3-4, 8).

The arrival of a teaching priest provoked a complete change of story and also imparted courage. At a point, King Asa was discouraged, but when the teaching priest interpreted those scriptures, life virtues entered into him; courage came and strength was built up. With courage, we subdue oppositions and secure our destinies.

And they sware unto the LORD with a loud voice,

> ***and with shouting, and with trumpets, and with cornets.***
>
> ***And all Judah rejoiced at the oath: for they had sworn with all their heart, and sought him with their whole desire; and he was found of them: and the LORD gave them rest round about.***
>
> *2 Chronicles 15:14-15*

Therefore, by the ministry of the teaching priest, we take spiritual command to compel our all-round rest. Just a word from the Lord through a teaching priest, can change any situation, if we open our hearts to receive it.

As it is written: ***For with thee is the fountain of life: in thy light shall we see light*** (Psalm 36:9).

In every generation, there are ordained persons through whom we see God's light. As it is written: ***I have also spoken by the prophets, and I have multiplied visions, and used similitudes, by the ministry of the prophets*** (Hosea 12:10).

God is still visiting people on the earth through the instrumentality of His priests as agents of rescue. This can be accessed through physical contacts, books and other resource materials. God gives us encounters with deeper understanding through the ministry of His anointed ones. Thus, we do not receive understanding by just hanging in their ministry, but by pressing into what they carry.

Concerning Uzziah, the Bible records in 2 Chronicles 26:5 that: ***...he sought God in the days of Zechariah, who had understanding in the visions of God: and as long as he sought the LORD, God made him to prosper***.

Uzziah enjoyed his turnaround through the ministry of Zechariah. He walked in the light that Zechariah had and enjoyed the same order of turnarounds he encountered. There are people through whom we encounter light, via the light they have encountered.

There are things we may never understand without God guiding us through someone. There are people sent our way to boost our spiritual understanding. God said, "...I will give you pastors according to mine heart which shall feed you with knowledge and understanding" (Jeremiah 3:15). That means, through the ministry of those sent to us, we experience enlargement and this is a function of our understanding.

We benefit from the ministry of prophets through:

- Books
- Compact Disc (CDs)
- Direct word from God in a meeting or gathering of believers. When we receive a direct word from God, we are sure of it.

Therefore, we should sweep through the Scripture and

anointed books until we find what suits our situations. We also have to listen to CDs and tapes to contact our turnaround words.

The ministry of teaching priests is one ministry that many people have lost touch with, because they do not believe God can speak to them through that medium. He does not speak to us directly alone; He also speaks through whatever medium He chooses.

Many years ago, I had a dramatic encounter with the word of power through the ministry of Kenneth E. Hagin. God said to me: "My son, David, the baton has been passed over to you." God spoke to me through the ministry of that prophet, giving me the baton of the Word of Faith – a movement for this generation.

My life as an individual has been dramatically influenced by Christian literatures. I am largely a product of books. I believe my worth would have been far less than what it is today without access to life-changing books.

In 1976, I had two separate life-changing encounters with two Christian literatures that have remained assets to my Christian journey, till date. First, through a book titled, *The Purpose of Pentecost* written by Dr. T. L Osborn. I read the entire book in one sitting, and the hand of the Lord came heavily upon me and my spiritual ears popped open. For the first time, I heard the voice of God clearly.

It was this encounter that led to my understanding of my mission on earth. When the Liberation Mandate was delivered over 30 years ago, I was able to discern clearly between the voice of the Shepherd and the voice of the stranger. Till today, I hear God clearly as a man hears his friend on every vital issue of my life. What an asset that has been to my life and ministry.

Also, that same year, I encountered the mystery of dedication as the secret of life's fulfilment and assurance of eternity through a book titled, *The Man God Uses* by Oswald J. Smith. By that encounter, I entered into a covenant with God for a life of total commitment. I became dead to self and alive to God. As it is written, ***Except a corn of wheat falls to the ground, it abides alone. But if it dies, it brings forth much fruits*** (John 12:24).

I believe that encounter was a springboard to my fruitful adventure with Christ till date.

God speaks to us through the ministry of teaching priests. If we do not know what they carry, we will not position ourselves to connect with the flow of their prophetic ministry. Therefore, anointed books are boosters of spiritual understanding, which in turn puts us in command of the issues of life.

Attend to it and Qualify for it

Without genuine attention, we cannot get our sent

word. Triumphing in the world of command requires giving genuine attention to the Word. Many people do not have time for the issues of their lives; they keep waiting for that "one day". There is no such day! Every day is the Lord's Day, but the day we encounter our word is our day. We have to give attention to the Word to get what we desire.

As it is written: ***And ye shall seek me, and find me, when ye shall search for me with all your heart*** (Jeremiah 29:13).

The woman with the issue of blood did not wait for "one day"; if she had, she would have missed it for life. If Bartimaeus had waited for "one day", he would have died a blind man. Everyone that had an encounter with God went for it.

After we were instructed by God to move to Canaanland, I took time out to study the wilderness ministry of Jesus and how He was able to gather the crowd, even in the wilderness. My discovery fortified my faith. I knew that multitudes would gather, because of my encounter with the Word.

Therefore, when we are faced with any challenge, we should undertake a project of discovery by saying, "Lord, what is it that I need to do at this point?" Then, He will show us because whatsoever we ask, believing, shall be manifested to us. It takes a studious life to gain access to the Word of command.

> ***My son, attend to my words; incline thine ear unto my sayings. Let them not depart from thine eyes; keep them in the midst of thine heart. For they are life unto those that find them, and health to all their flesh.***
>
> *Proverbs 4:20-22*

If we don't give attention to the Word, we will not get it because the Word of command requires genuine attention of the seeker.

There was a lady who came for Shiloh 2007 from Ghana, because her body was ravaged by HIV/AIDs. After Shiloh, she purchased the tapes, travelled to Kwara State where she had some relatives and locked herself in a room for two weeks. After that, she went to the hospital for a test and the result was negative. Before then, she was at her dying point, but she gave attention to the Word and her turnaround came.

Therefore, we must accept responsibility to give attention to the word that will bring about our desired turnarounds. Our heart is the candle with which we search out whatever is missing in our lives through the Word. That is why only those who give attention to the Word ever get their breakthroughs.

Employ the Help of the Holy Spirit

The anointing of the Holy Spirit is the vital factor

to gaining access to the truth. We need the empowerment of the Holy Ghost to gain access to the deep things of God.

The Holy Spirit is the custodian of revelations. All of Scripture was inspired by Him; so, He is in the best position to guide us through our search for a turnaround word. Interestingly, we cannot find our words with our minds; it can only be found with our spirits. God is bigger than our minds and intellect. If God ever comes into our intellect, it will blow up.

Our intellect has no capacity to access, retain or utilise mysteries. Therefore, we need to engage our spirits. The manifestation of the supernatural is always sequel to the outpouring of the Holy Ghost. Thus, we must employ the help of the Holy Spirit, or we will never manifest as signs on the earth. There is no way our minds can accommodate divine mysteries; it is beyond our natural self. We need to be able to distinguish between our spirits and our souls, in order to seek God with our hearts (Proverbs 4:20-23).

It is with the help of the Holy Ghost that we encounter our Word of change. We need to know that the search is not intellectual but spiritual. The Bible says: ***With my soul have I desired thee in the night; yea, with my spirit within me will I seek thee early…*** (Isaiah 26:9; see also Romans 8:16).

Therefore, we need our spirit to commune with the Spirit of God in order to access the precious seeds for our desired turnaround. Anyone can access the stories of the Scripture, whether saved or unsaved, but only men and women of the Spirit can access the seed of the Word; and we need that seed for a turnaround experience.

Many read the Bible but do not connect with the mysteries in it. As stated earlier, the things that make for our turnarounds are not on the surface, but in the deep and only the Holy Ghost can take us to the "deep". When we connect to His erudite teaching ministry, He brings us to the depth of His Word.

Pray and Fast

This is a sure access to Rhema from the Word. If we need a word of command, we must commit ourselves to a lifestyle of prayer. When we read the Bible for direction, we must ask for the Holy Spirit's help and the result can be attained speedily when we engage in a fast.

He said: ***Call unto me, and I will answer thee, and shew thee great and mighty things, which thou knowest not*** (Jeremiah 33:3).

That is why Jesus said, "When ye pray..., when ye fast;" not "if" you pray or "if" you fast. Prayer and fasting are supposed to be part of our life programmes. We may ask why? It is because we need light at all times.

When Daniel and his friends engaged in prayers, the secret was revealed to Daniel in a night vision. It was a turnaround revelation without which he would have been dead with the other magicians. They were all to be killed, but he got a turnaround revelation through prayers (Daniel 2:16-19).

Our engagement in prayer and fasting also boosts our spiritual status. We discover from the Scripture that those who embark on spiritual adventures naturally capture their future from the Word. Therefore, engage in spiritual adventures, not sightseeing!

> ***Then shall thy light break forth as the morning, and thine health shall spring forth speedily: and thy righteousness shall go before thee; the glory of the LORD shall be thy rearward.***
>
> *Isaiah 58:8*

Fasting is a spiritual medium through which we experience the breaking forth of light. When we fast, we are away from the body and present with God. Our spirit-man becomes receptive to signals from heaven. Fasting brings us closer to God and because He dwells in light where no man can approach, the light breaks forth in our lives.

In March 1984, when the key to supernatural church growth was handed over to me, I was alert to receive it. Since then, I saw unlimited crowds everywhere. Thus, fasting makes our spirit-man alert to God.

Paul said: ***For this cause we also, since the day we heard it, do not cease to pray for you, and to desire that ye might be filled with the knoweldge of his will in all wisdom and spiritual understanding*** (Colossians 1:9).

Also, Solomon prayed, and God gave him wisdom, understanding and largeness of heart more than the sand on the seashore. We can pray for spiritual understanding, but it is fasting that empowers our prayer. Through fasting, we can experience the breaking forth of light that terminates struggles. It guarantees a breaking forth that cannot be doubted forever.

Fasting is ordained for our empowerment. Remember the Bible says that the yoke shall be destroyed because of the anointing. When Jesus went on a fasting spree, He returned in the power of the Spirit. When we are empowered, we are enthroned and our territories are enlarged (Isaiah 10:27; Mark 1:28).

We Must Search with our Hearts

> ***With my soul have I desired thee in the night; yea, with my spirit within me will I seek thee early: for when thy judgments are in the earth, the inhabitants***

of the world will learn righteousness.

Isaiah 26:9

We set the pace with a desire in mind, but we actually get the fullness of God and the deep revelations of His Word by our spirit. Too many people seek God with their heads, when they can only find Him with their hearts. Locating God's plan for our lives requires a hearty search.

And ye shall seek me, and find me, when ye shall search for me with all your heart.

Jeremiah 29:13

Most people have not found it, even when they think they have. What they have found are stories but what I am referring to are mysteries. When we find someone talking about his discovery from the Scriptures, that means he has found it.

We cannot discover God with our minds. It is impossible to capture His ways with our human instincts. We can only connect with God with our spirits and our hearts.

Remember the Bible says: ***The spirit of man is the candle of the LORD, searching all the inward parts of the belly*** (Proverbs 20:27).

This Scripture encourages us to light up our spirit and engage it in a search, in order to find answers to every bugging issue of our lives. We must sweep diligently until we find what we need.

We can only locate God's agenda with our spirit. To locate our turnaround Word, Jesus said, light a candle, sweep thoroughly, and we will find it. A man's spirit is that candle of the Lord that searches and draws from the depth of man (Proverbs 20:27). These things cannot be found naturally.

Be Meek

> ***The meek will he guide in judgment: and the meek will he teach his way.***
>
> *Psalm 25:9*

The meek will He teach in the way that He shall choose. It takes meekness to access dimensions of revelations in God. Moses was said to be the meekest of all men on the face of the earth, and there was no one that had any deeper revelation than Moses in the whole of the Old Testament.

The quality of our meekness determines the limits of our access. This has nothing to do with our pious looks, but how meekly we are in heart. Moses knew how God created man by revelation; he knew how God created the animals by revelation, and he knew how God began His journey. Five books of the Bible were delivered to him by revelation.

Jesus said: ***Come unto me, all ye that labour and***

are heavy laden, and I will give you rest. Take my yoke upon you, and learn of me; for I am meek and lowly in heart: and ye shall find rest unto your souls (Matthew 11:28-29).

If we want to access God, we need meekness. The meeker we are, the freer our access to the deep things of God. God will always resist the proud, so He can give more grace to the humble (James 4:6).

Be Filled with Joy

It takes joy to connect with water from the wells of salvation; and if we are referring to a well, every attempt to draw water is likened to a bucket. The rope we need to let down the bucket to the well is joy. No matter how much water is in a well, if we don't have a rope, a bucket is of no benefit to us.

Similarly, there are many "ropeless" Christians today, who are constantly depressed. Every little thing breaks their heart, just like little children weep over minute things. We can't remain as babies; we must grow up. Therefore, we need to rejoice!

The devil knows that we cannot access revelation with a broken heart; thus, he specialises in breaking our hearts, so we won't know the way out.

Paul the Apostle said: ***Rejoice in the Lord alway: and again I say, Rejoice.*** He also said, "Rejoice evermore," and Paul was a man of unusual revelation because he was a man addicted to joy. His joy was intoxicating (Philippians 4:4; 1 Thessalonians 5:16). The Bible says:

> ***Ye shall have a song, as in the night when a holy solemnity is kept; and gladness of heart, as when one goeth with a pipe to come into the mountain of the LORD, to the mighty One of Israel. And the LORD shall cause his glorious voice to be heard, and shall shew the lighting down of his arm, with the indignation of his anger, and with the flame of a devouring fire, with scattering, and tempest, and hailstones. For through the voice of the LORD shall the Assyrian be beaten down, which smote with a rod.***
>
> *Isaiah 30:29-31*

Revelation demands jubilation. God's voice is a joyful voice; so, only a joyful heart can connect with it. He said: ***Thou wilt shew me the path of life: in thy presence is fulness of joy; at thy right hand there are pleasures for evermore*** (Psalm 16:11).

Therefore, to get the Word for our turnarounds, we must arrive in His presence with joy and that is where He can show us the path of life. Every time we carry a long face, it shows that we have a long way to go. Hence, to get our instant turnarounds, we need joy that flows from the heart.

Be Still

Be still, and know that I am God: I will be exalted among the heathen, I will be exalted in the earth.

Psalm 46:10

We must be still because the voice of the Lord is a still small voice. Elijah was out in the cave and there was an earthquake, a strong wind, and fire but God was not there, until there was a still small voice (1 Kings 19:9-13).

Our access to the right and sent Word will only come to us if we are still and not when we are troubled. The more peaceful we are, the more insightful we become.

It is only when we are peaceful and our minds are at rest that our ears can hear a word behind us, saying: ***This is the way, walk ye in it, when ye turn to the right hand, and when ye turn to the left*** (Isaiah 30:21).

The more troubled we are, the more disconnected we become. The more peaceful we are, the more insight we gain. Therefore, I say to every storm in your life, peace be still!

FIVE

POWER OF REVELATION

The entrance of thy words giveth light, it giveth understanding unto the simple.

Psalm 119:130

The Word of God is the master key to a world of all-round breakthroughs; but the spiritual understanding of it is what empowers the Word to maximally deliver our desired expectations. The Word delivers only to the measure of our understanding of it, because it is that understanding that converts the Word to light.

Think about it: it is impossible to gain from anything without an understanding of what that thing is made for and how it can be applied. Therefore, it is the understanding of the Word that pertains to our situations that puts us in command. It is written that all things were created by the Word and there is nothing that we see that was made outside the creative power of the Word. That means, there is no situation that desires a turnaround that is not under the command of the Word (John 1:3; Hebrews 1:3).

However, until we see what has been written concerning our desired change, our frustration on that issue continues. This is why what we see and believe from the Scripture concerning ourselves, determines the outcome of our destinies.

Revelation of the Word is all about being able to see what God is saying concerning a particular situation. That simply means, spiritual understanding of the Word is the bedrock for exploits, because revelation is the unveiling of Kingdom mysteries, which empowers us for mastery.

The Bible is made up of stories but inside the stories of the Scriptures are mysteries. These stories can be accessed intellectually, but the realm of mysteries can only be accessed spiritually. The stories are powerless; they cannot change anybody's life. It is the mystery that changes our lives and that is the importance of revelation.

Jesus said that it is given to us to know the mysteries

of the Kingdom (revelation) and as we all know, we perish for lack of it. It is impossible for us to realise God's agenda of continuous advancement, except by revelation (Mark 4:11; Hosea 4:6).

Revelation makes a revolutionary of the beneficiary. We are turned into "another man" by light, because our destinies are limited by our insight. The farther we see, the farther we go. Spiritual understanding is our greatest asset as believers in the journey of life and it is the level of understanding that differentiates one believer from another. Spiritual understanding is what gives value to any other thing we have, because revelation changes our levels unendingly.

> ***But the path of the just is as the shining light, that shineth more and more unto the perfect day.***
>
> *Proverbs 4:18*

More often than not, our torments and struggles are traceable to inadequate revelation to deal with the issues confronting us. Revelation of the Word is what re-engineers our mentality.

The devil is not powerful; we are just victims of ignorance. It is the absence of our personal light from the Scripture that gives him power over us. When we have the revelation concerning the situation confronting us, we are free and in charge, because it is the light of the Word that empowers us for liberty, exploits and total turnarounds.

All through the Scriptures, we discover that men and women of revelation were people of all-round breakthroughs. Pharaoh said to Joseph, "Forasmuch as God hath shewed thee all this..." (Genesis 41:38-44). That's revelation! Daniel was also a man of deep revelation that he gained insight into what the king dreamt in his bed and also had the interpretation of it. He also acknowledged the fact that there is a God in heaven that reveals secrets. By revelation, he became a father and a god to the king (Daniel 2:28, 46).

All men of insights are men of exploits. Job was also a man of great insight because he said, "As I was in the days of my youth, when the secret of God was upon my tabernacle" (Job 29:4). His revelation and love for God made him the greatest of all men in the East, in his days. Even in his capacity, he had the insight of what to do and that gave him a change of story.

One light from heaven brought us into realms of financial fortune as a ministry. I never heard the revelation of what I got from the Word taught anywhere in my life. God visited me in the early hours of September 4, 1987 and said: "The same way I open the heavens over individuals, I open the heavens over corporations, organisations, institutions, including churches." That came like lightning and set me upon my feet. It was not an ordinary revelation, because it brought us into an unending realm of financial fortune.

Revelation always makes the difference, because God is no respecter of persons. There is nothing the gospel has produced in any place or in any man's life that cannot be reproduced. Revelation is no respecter of nations; wherever light shines, darkness backs off. It commands the same authority anywhere under the sun.

The problem is not in the nation we live in, or the occupation that we engage in, it is the inadequate illumination to dominate our situations. Nothing dominates life situations like divine illuminations.

It is written: ***And the light shineth in darkness; and the darkness comprehended it not*** (John 1:5).

It is also written: ***Wisdom is the principal thing; therefore get wisdom: and with all thy getting get understanding*** (Proverbs 4:7).

We need the Spirit of wisdom and revelation in order to grow from intellectualism to inspiration. The wisdom the Bible is talking about in the above scripture is intellectual. We need to secure intellectualism, but beyond that, we need to get understanding. That was what differentiated Daniel and his colleagues, from others (Daniel 1:17-20).

We must understand that we live in a Kingdom that operates on keys and these keys are the revelations we catch from the Word to deal with any issue that confronts us. Without the right key, we keep struggling around circumstances. When we get the right Word concerning any area of concern to us, God is committed to turning that situation around and when He is committed, every mountain crumbles.

The Effect of Revelation

The revelation of the truth is the master key to a world of dominion. All our inheritances are in the Bible, and when we can see our turnarounds and believe what the Word says concerning any situation, we are empowered to become what the Word says. As it is written: ***But as many as received him, to them gave he power to become the sons of God, even to them that believe on his name*** (John 1:12). Remember, God said to Abraham that as far as his eyes could see, unto him would He give it (Genesis 13:14-15).

Everything we need to live the "heaven on earth" kind of life is in the Word, but we need the Spirit of wisdom and revelation to help us see the reality of our inheritances in the Word of God.

People with deep revelations are restful because they are filled with faith, which makes them surer of tomorrow than even today. They have seen the realities of their tomorrow, so they cannot be roughened by circumstances today.

The Bible enjoins us to ***look unto Jesus the author and finisher of our faith; who for the joy that was set before him endured the cross, despising the shame, and is set down at the right hand of the throne of God*** (Hebrews 12:2).

Nothing is sweeter than the revelation of the Word. It puts us in command of the situations of life. By revelation, I dominated madness. Some years back, I was basking in the revelation of John chapter one, when I was informed that my cousin was accosted by the spirit of insanity. With the revelation I got from that chapter, I knew I had dominated the situation, so I waited till I was through with the family meeting. When I got to where he was kept, he prostrated to greet me.

When asked if he knew me, he said: "He is my brother." Before then, he did not recognise anyone including his mother. Then, I instructed them to "put him in the car, let me see the devil that will follow him into my car." When we are thoroughly illuminated, we dominate without struggles. When we encounter adequate light concerning our health, sickness will be far from our dwellings.

> ***Truly the light is sweet, and a pleasant thing it is for the eyes to behold the sun.***
>
> *Ecclesiastes 11:7*

There is nothing peculiar about your case, don't let the devil make you think that your case is special. There is no special darkness; when light comes every form of darkness disappears. When I encountered light from the ministry of Smith Wigglesworth on my supremacy over devils, I became wild. That revelation is still in me!

It is revelation that engraces us for exploits. The Bible says:

> ***Arise, shine; for thy light is come, and the glory of the Lord is risen upon thee. For, behold, the darkness shall cover the earth, and gross darkness the people: but the Lord shall arise upon thee, and his glory shall be seen upon thee. And the Gentiles shall come to thy light, and kings to the brightness of thy rising.***
>
> *Isaiah 60:1-3*

By redemption, we are ordained for global impact. We are sent to be blessings to all the families of the earth. However, we must be able to see it, because if it is too much for our minds, it will be too much for our hands. If we cannot imagine our turnarounds, we cannot see them. As the seeds of Abraham, we are among the people ordained to be blessings to all the families of the earth.

> ***And I will bless them that bless thee, and curse him that curseth thee: and in thee shall all families of***

the earth be blessed.

Genesis 12:3

And if ye be Christ's, then are ye Abraham's seed, and heirs according to the promise.

Galatians 3:29

If we belong to Christ, we are men and women of exploits by redemption, and revelation is the gateway to the actualisation of our exploits.

A young man came to my office years ago to complain to me that he had no job. When he related his story to me, I showed him Isaiah 3:10 that says: ***Say ye to the righteous, that it shall be well with him: for they shall eat the fruit of their doings.***

Immediately, light dawned on him and darkness gave way. I saw faith in him, so I said, "Go get a job" and he got a miracle job almost immediately. The righteous is not permitted to be a burden to anyone; we are expected to earn a living.

Revelation enhances our spiritual weight. We have to get to a point where we can receive a word that will give us the confidence to tell anyone about our turnaround. It is that type of revelation that terminates barrenness, joblessness, poverty and every ugly situation in our lives. We will be able to declare our change of status without any iota of doubt in us, because we are propelled by revelation.

We cannot stop saying what we have seen, because what we are unable to say, we do not truly have a revelation of. We may be confused or harassed when declaring the information we have heard, but when it comes to what we have seen, we can boldly declare it. When the Apostles were confronted, they said:

> ***For we cannot but speak the things which we have seen and heard.***
>
> *Acts 4:20*

No matter the circumstances that surround us, when light comes, our turnaround is certain. The degree to which we enjoy our inheritances in God is determined by our depth of revelation, which is the security of our destiny. Therefore, we must have adequate revelation!

Proofs of Revelation of the Word

Supernatural Faith is Stirred

Every time revelation dawns, faith rises because we cannot see a thing and doubt it. When faith is stirred, supernatural victory is guaranteed. We can dare anything when we see the light.

As it is written: ***Open thou mine eyes, that I may behold wondrous things out of thy law*** (Psalm 119:18).

Until our eyes are open to the revelation of the truth, we cannot believe, and until we believe, we cannot see the manifestation of God's glory in our lives. Therefore, revelation makes us go beyond hearing God's Word to seeing our future in it, and then becoming what the Word says.

Men of revelation are men of faith, and every man of faith is more than a conqueror, because he can quench all the fiery darts of the enemy (Ephesians 6:16).

Confidence is Boosted

> ***...but the people that do know their God shall be strong, and do exploits.***
>
> *Daniel 11:32*

Revelation boosts confidence, which is required to take command. Confidence is the conqueror's backbone and the security of our inheritances in Christ. That is why our confidence is the target of the enemy in battle. Therefore, it is important to build and sustain our confidence in God and this can only be through adequate revelation.

> ***Cast not away therefore your confidence, which hath great recompence of reward.***
>
> *Hebrews 10:35*

Unperturbed Peace

"Peace" here means rest. People of revelation are never disturbed, no matter what happens.

> ***Great peace have they which love thy law: and nothing shall offend them.***
>
> *Psalm 119:165*

Knowledge, which equals revelation, is the channel for peace and the deeper the revelation, the calmer we are. A number of times, people have asked me, "Why do you smile at all times?" I tell them that it is because I know what to do!

When we walk in revelation, we find ourselves living continuously in peace. As it is written: ***Grace and peace be multiplied unto you through the knowledge of God, and of Jesus our Lord*** (2 Peter 1:2).

Jesus was calm in the midst of the storm because He knew what to do by reason of the revelation He had. His disciples were apprehensive but He slept, because He knew from the Word that He could never be molested by any circumstance or force of nature.

There is a kind of peace that revelation brings that keeps our hearts and minds focused on Christ Jesus. That is the peace of God that passes all understanding. It is an unexplainable peace that flows like a river; it is peace beyond disturbance, above anxieties and it can be felt by all.

The Bible enjoins us to labour in order to enter into that rest, for the Word of God is quick and powerful. Therefore, when we labour in the Word by searching tirelessly until we encounter revelation, our faith comes alive and that gives us supernatural rest (Hebrews 4:11-12).

It Enhances the Quality of our Results

The level of revelation we have concerning an issue determines the degree of our dominion. The revelation of the truth, when embraced, produces undeniable proofs. Revelation changes our levels unendingly. Our torments and struggles are traceable to our limited insight. This is because we lack adequate revelation to deal with the issues confronting us.

Talking about the parable of the sower, which yielded different levels of results based on the different levels of understanding; some bore fruits 100 fold, some 60 and some 30. Thus, the more we understand, the better enhanced our blessings and results.

> ***But he that received seed into the good ground is he that heareth the word, and understandeth it; which also beareth fruit, and bringeth forth, some an hundredfold, some sixty, some thirty.***
>
> *Matthew 13:23*

From the above scripture, those who heard the Word had good and honest hearts, but they had varied depth of understanding, which determined their level of productivity. Therefore, our turnaround is a function of our spiritual understanding.

Unending Joy

Anyone flowing in revelation automatically and naturally flows in joy. We cannot flow in revelation and still be tormented by depression. Revelation triggers the joy of the Lord in us.

> ***Thy words were found, and I did eat them; and thy word was unto me the joy and rejoicing of mine heart: for I am called by thy name, O Lord God of hosts.***
>
> *Jeremiah 15:16*

The Word of God, when revealed, triggers joy unspeakable, full of glory. Therefore, deep revelation triggers addictive joy that we cannot be separated from, and it cannot be tied to anything natural.

Depression puts God off and brings the devil in. So, we must make a choice. We cannot enter into His gates without thanksgiving or into His courts without praise. We cannot be in His presence without fullness of joy. Depression is a design of the devil to separate us from God. It is written: ***Rejoice in the Lord alway: and again I say, Rejoice*** (Philippians 4:4).

Divine Health

My son, attend to my words; incline thine ear unto my sayings. Let them not depart from thine eyes; keep them in the midst of thine heart. For they are life unto those that find them, and health to all their flesh.

Proverbs 4:20-22

More revelation is equal to more strength, and more strength equals more exploits. It takes revelation to enjoy increasing strength. The more revelation at work in us, the more strength we are able to manifest and that qualifies us for more exploits. There is no man of exploits that will not require strength and supernatural stamina.

We need strength and stamina to command exploits, and men of insights are men of unusual exploits. Moses was a man of unusual insight and he had unusual strength. At the age of 80, he went on a 40-day fast continually to renew his strength. He had unusual vigour. This shows that the level of revelation we have, determines the level of strength we command.

It is written:

A wise man is strong; yea, a man of knowledge increaseth strength (Proverbs 24:5; see also Daniel 11:32).

Supernatural Exploits

By revelation, we command the attention of kings. It is a flight that is powered by light. There are human beings who are nations. Thus, a small one can be turned into a strong nation by revelation. As it is written:

> ***Arise, shine; for thy light is come, and the glory of the LORD is risen upon thee.***
>
> ***For, behold, the darkness shall cover the earth, and gross darkness the people: but the LORD shall arise upon thee, and his glory shall be seen upon thee.***
>
> ***And the Gentiles shall come to thy light, and kings to the brightness of thy rising.***
>
> ***Who are these that fly as a cloud, and as the doves to their windows?***
>
> ***A little one shall become a thousand, and a small one a strong nation: I the LORD will hasten it in his time.***
>
> *Isaiah 60:1-3, 8, 22*

This implies that by reason of the revelation we encounter, men of honour and dignity will accord us respect. Revelation places us above the ordinary level and brings us to a level where we begin to marvel at our flight. We must also understand that revelation not only brings us honour, it also changes our position and fortifies our walls.

Joseph was released from prison by revelation and that repositioned him as the leader of a nation. Egypt was the strongest nation of that time and by revelation, he was placed on top. Also, by revelation, the four captives in Babylon became the rulers of the land. Daniel was at the centre of it and Shadrach, Meshach and Abednego ruled at the provincial level. Therefore, adequate revelation makes rulers out of us.

Revelation is the power base for transformation, because when we have access to unending renewal, we encounter unending transformations. Therefore, the deeper our realms of revelation, the greater our level of turnarounds.

It is, therefore, important for us to seek adequate knowledge of what we do not know and stop celebrating what we know. This is because what we know determines where we are; but if we know better, we will change levels. The struggles of our lives are not products of what we earn, but our lack of adequate light.

SIX

QUALITY WORD STUDY

Till I come, give attendance to reading, to exhortation, to doctrine.

Meditate upon these things; give thyself wholly to them; that thy profiting may appear to all.

1 Timothy 4:13 & 15

The weight of a substance determines the depth of the sound it makes when it lands on the ground. Our impact is a function of our spiritual weight and this is what defines our practice. This weight is achieved through in-depth study of the Word.

Where we stand with the Word today determines our

place tomorrow, because everything in life answers to the Word and everything was made by the Word (John 1:1-3).

We must know that our lives can be transformed through studying. This is because whether written or spoken, the value of words cannot be adequately quantified. Words either make or break destinies. That is why God gave us His Word as a roadmap to guide us through the journey of life.

Therefore, our study of His Word determines our victory in life. It is Word depth that determines Word impact, and Word explosion is the trigger for all supernatural manifestations. When we apply ourselves to the depth of God's Word as unfolded to us, and we prove it in our lives, our profiting will appear to all.

As it is written: ***Study to shew thyself approved unto God, a workman that needeth not to be ashamed, rightly dividing the word of truth*** (2 Timothy 2:15).

We must study the Word effectively if we do not want to be downcast or ashamed. The Bible clearly states that when we seek, we shall find. Thus, the answer to our challenges is in seeking the Word for appropriate solutions.

The Art of Studying

The art of studying involves a conscious search for

facts that have to do with our needs. We search the Word for heavenly information that will ultimately produce earthly transformations. When we commit to Word study, we search with the intent of finding something of benefit that will change our lives forever. It is a committed study that makes Christian living profitable.

Some years ago, the Holy Spirit said to me, "Learning is richer than praying; learning has greater value than fasting. Learning is the master key to living." What it takes to get what we want from the Word is far cheaper than the challenge we are going through.

Many years ago, I was desperate to find the mystery of Kingdom prosperity. Thus, I read the books, *The Laws of Prosperity* and *God's Will is Prosperity* by Kenneth and Gloria Copeland respectively. I searched desperately like someone who had lost something and must find it, and I did that while in a three-day fast.

At the end of that exercise, my understanding broadened, my spirit-man caught fresh fire and I had spiritual insight on the subject matter. With that, I spun around and screamed, "I can never be poor!" Through that encounter, God delivered me from poverty and gave me command over financial issues forever.

We can gain command over any issue of concern through the Word and this can only come by the revelation of the truth, which we encounter in quality Word study. We might have been struggling with some issues; it does not matter the years they have lingered, all we need is an encounter with the Word. Engaging in targeted study helps us encounter light that will enable us dominate those issues.

However, we must note that the main purpose of our study is to show ourselves approved of God. It is when we show ourselves approved of God that we have proofs, which culminates in our turnarounds.

To rightly divide the Word of truth is to know which scripture is most appropriate to handle a particular challenge; that means, having a revelation of the right word to produce our desired turnarounds. Being supernaturally in control of the issues of life is not a function of chance, but of choice. Until we choose to know how to get what we desire from the Word, our struggles continue.

I remember when the spirit of death accosted our last daughter, I had to seek a quiet time with God to get a solution over that issue. I said, "Lord, there must be a way out." He gave me four scriptures that dominated that challenge. He said to me from Revelation chapter 1 verse 18, "I am He that was dead and behold I am alive and I live forever more and I have the keys of hell and of death in My hand; and I am holding that key in favour of My children." That scripture came from a quality Word study.

Therefore, it is the quality of the Word in us, which comes from adequate Word study, that defines the happenings in and around us. When we throw a stone into water, the size of the stone is what determines the spread of the ripples on the face of the water. It is the same with the Word, with regards to tackling the issues that confront us.

For instance, Daniel was a studious man, because he said he understood by books and through that understanding, he had insights that made him important to four governments in his time, even in captivity. Nothing can take the place of a studious life; not even our gift or anointing.

Paul was also a man with great unction, but he could not do without studying. He said: ***The cloke that I left at Troas with Carpus, when thou comest, bring with thee, and the books, but especially the parchments*** (2 Timothy 4:13).

Therefore, constant study of the Word and application of it is key to our desired change. What we derive from the Word addresses all issues of life and answers every bugging question that may confront us. That is why no student of the Word is a failure.

A lady was stagnated in her career and according to her: *In September 2011, I got a temporary appointment.*

In that organisation, I met so many temporary staff who had stayed up to nine years. However, I told myself that my own case is different.

In April 2012, a lady in my office resigned and I was posted to her office. I kept declaring Psalm 75 verses 6 and 7, and I stood upon this Word from where I caught light! Few days after Shiloh 2012, I was called to receive my permanent appointment letter. I give all the praise to God! **–Betty, I. E.**

Whatever we need, can be obtained from our knowledge of the Word. Until we find it in the Word, it cannot be fulfilled in our lives. It is, therefore, necessary to give adequate attention to Word study.

We Must Search with our Hearts

A studious Christian is triumphant at all times. Until God's Word gains control over us, we won't gain command over the circumstances of life. The Word is powerful, but labouring fervently in it is the pathway to having all our needs met.

When studying the Word, we need to search as someone looking for a lost item. Most times, people give up searching, when it seems as if they cannot see what they are searching for. It is important to note that until we get our word, our turnaround is not in view. Nothing commits God to perform like discovered truth. Once we find it, God will confirm it, because He cannot deny Himself.

Also, to get the best from Word study, we need to engage the Holy Spirit in prayer. He is our God-ordained Teacher and He compares spiritual things with spiritual. The Bible is a spiritual text, so we can only get anything from it when we approach it from a spiritual angle, which is through the help of the Holy Spirit.

While growing up, I saw some disheartening issues in marriage that prompted me to ask God about His purpose for instituting marriage. In my in-depth search of the Scriptures and meditation, I discovered seven power keys to a hitch-free marriage. Thus, Word study provides answers to every area of concern in one's life.

To gain relevant substance from the Word and not mere stories, we must be spiritually minded and we are either spiritual or carnal; we cannot be neutral. The more spiritually disposed we are, the greater our access to revelation. Therefore, all kinds of junk jesting, careless telephone calls and misuse of time must stop (Romans 8:6).

Engage in a Spirited Search, not an Intellectual Search

With my soul have I desired thee in the night; yea, with my spirit within me will I seek thee early: for

when thy judgments are in the earth, the inhabitants of the world will learn righteousness.

Isaiah 26:9

The spirit of a man is the candle of the Lord. Spiritual things can only be found by the Spirit. Thus, it takes a spirited search to access the deep things of God; because "deep calleth unto the deep." It is our spirit that connects us with the Spirit of God to bring us into the deep things of God. This is so important. We must engage our spirit in the search (Proverbs 20:27; Psalm 42:1-3).

Commit to Diligent Study

Study to shew thyself approved unto God, a work man that needeth not to be ashamed, rightly dividing the word of truth (2 Timothy 2:15).

We cannot get the right Word for a change except we are studious, and a thorough search can be empowered by the Spirit of wisdom and revelation. Our inheritances are in the Bible, and the Holy Spirit helps us to see them when we engage Him in a meaningful search. Consequently, when we see our word and we believe it, we are empowered to become it (John 1:12).

Apostle Paul was a man who had passion for books; he constantly checked and searched through books. He said: ***The cloak that I left at Troas with Carpus,***

when thou comest, bring with thee, and the books, but especially the parchments (2 Timothy 4:13).

We cannot find these things while sleeping. When a student is about to write an examination, we encourage him to "sit up". This is because we don't lie down to pass an examination; we sit up!

Nothing is sweeter than accessing revelation because it puts us in command of the situations of life. When we are thoroughly illuminated, we dominate without struggles. When we encounter adequate light from our search of the Word, we keep flying.

There is nothing peculiar about our case; therefore, we should not allow the devil to make us feel as if our case is special. There is no special darkness; when light comes, every form of darkness disappears.

Apostle Paul said: ***Till I come, give attendance to reading, to exhortation, to doctrine. Meditate upon these things; give thyself wholly to them; that thy profiting may appear to all*** (1 Timothy 4:13, 15).

Today, our ministry enjoys an unusual church growth, but it sprang from highly explorative studies of the ministry of Yonggi Cho in South Korea in 1985. We still use his materials today in growing our cell system.

It is important to understand that the word of command cannot be accessed without a studious life. We must search for answers to bugging questions in our lives from the Bible and books from anointed authors. The word of command does not drop on a man's lap; we have to go for it.

I had a word of command on marriage, because I went for it. I am over 30 years young in it, and it is sweet because I have command over it. It was so authentic and valid that I said: "It is going to be a hitch-free adventure."

Daniel was a studious man. He said ***...I Daniel understood by books...*** (Daniel 9:2). Even though he was gifted, it was his studious life that boosted the gift of God in him; otherwise, his gift would have lost its potency.

We must embark on destiny projects the same way we do to building projects. There are issues tormenting our lives; are we going to watch them forever? We do not necessarily need money to be free from them; we just need to be spiritually responsible.

Ruminate on the Word

In most cases, inspiration works through the channel of meditation. Everyone who desires a change of level must be a thinker. We must be able to ruminate on the Word to get the Holy Spirit inspired meaning of it.

It entails "chewing on" the Word until we get the nutrients out of the same. It is the nutrients in the

Word that we need, to diffuse every issue confronting us. Although the Word is the master key to all circumstances of life, we need to stay on it, feed on it, and allow it to control our lives.

It is written: ***Through desire a man, having separated himself, seeketh and intermeddleth with all wisdom*** (Proverbs 18:1).

To experience unending change of levels as believers, we must engage our minds in the Word. That involves using the Word to evaluate the issues that confront us, so we can come up with practical answers.

When we meditate on the Word, we take delivery of our desires and when we equally give ourselves to what we have found, it profits us.

We cannot engage in qualitative meditation or have access to revelation if all we do is receive unending calls and watch all the programmes on television. We need to spend time with the Word, through the help of the Holy Spirit, to access our turnarounds.

SEVEN

POWER OF MEDITATION

This book of the law shall not depart out of thy mouth; but thou shalt meditate therein day and night, that thou mayest observe to do according to all that is written therein: for then thou shalt make thy way prosperous, and then thou shalt have good success.

Joshua 1:8

The mind can be seen as the control room of man's life because it coordinates and determines its activities. How much we get from life is a function of how well we engage our minds in productive activities. Great accomplishments are reserved for those who think.

Men of impact are men of great revelations and these come through constant meditation. Man's brain is the means behind his accomplishments; it is the live wire of his destiny; but it does not produce great profit automatically. It must be adequately engaged in the right way to bring about transformational results.

As we expose our minds to the right Word for our desired turnarounds, our faith is built and our change is certain. Through meditation, we generate divine authority to gain absolute command over the issues of life. Meditation equally produces life-changing inspiration and destiny-moulding revelations. Furthermore, through meditation, we are provoked by supernatural reflections to generate success secrets in life.

For instance, a young lady came to me years ago and told me that she got blank during her examination, so she did not write anything. I did not utter a word, but thought within me that there must be a way out.

In the course of my meditation, a word dropped in my spirit, "God has a pen! If He wrote the Ten Commandments with His hand, He must have a pen." I reasoned further that all things lay bare before God, so He must know where the young lady's paper was. Having acquired that insight, I said to her "God has a pen and if the Almighty is invisible, then, His pen is infinitesimally invisible; He can reach anywhere to fill up anything that He wants to fill up." She believed and as a result, she passed that examination. Today, several others have passed their examinations through that revelation, which came directly by meditation.

It is not enough to study, it is important to think and ponder on the Word. Meditation is key to accessing the deep things of God. It entails thinking through the word sent to us. It is seeing through every detail of the Word of God as it applies to our situations.

Many years ago, a woman came to me crying, because the doctor said she had no womb. I meditated in the Holy Ghost, and He said to me, "The thief cometh not but to steal, kill and destroy but I have come to replace." He said there is no manufacturer without a spare part store. I heard it from God in my meditation. Immediately, I gave her that word and it built her faith. Nine months later, she came back with her child.

All these testimonies validate the fact that we need meditation to access the mysteries in the Word. By meditation, I mean pondering on every word in the Scripture that addresses our desired turnarounds, so we can access the hidden treasures in it.

Habakkuk said: ***I will stand upon my watch, and set me upon the tower, and will watch to see what he will say unto me, and what I shall answer when I am***

reproved (Habakkuk 2:1).

The prodigal son meditated his way out of poverty. He reasoned within himself that the servants in his father's house had enough to feed on and give out; therefore, he could not remain in want. Through this, he concluded that if he could return to his father and ask for forgiveness, his challenge would be solved and it paid off. Through meditation, his dignity was restored.

David also meditated his way into deep understanding. He said: ***O how love I thy law! It is my meditation all the day. Thou through thy commandments hast made me wiser than mine enemies: for they are ever with me. I have more understanding than all my teachers: for thy testimonies are my meditation. I understand more than the ancients, because I keep thy precepts*** (Psalm 119:97-100).

David discovered the secret of meditation and that enhanced his productivity. As long as he gave himself to meditation, he had access to the deep things of God and that culminated in an enviable life.

God says so many things, but not everyone picks them. Until we can picture our desired turnaround from the Word, it is not secured. We only secure what we have seen. Many hear the Word, but cannot see through it. Our God is committed to doing exceedingly abundantly, above all that we ask or think.

There is always a seeing or hearing dimension to God's Word. Thus, we must picture our future from the Scripture, so it does not rupture.

Even the Word admonishes that we give attendance to reading, to exhortation and to doctrine. When we meditate on our found Word, our profiting will be seen by all (1 Timothy 4:13-14).

We need meditation to assimilate the truth so we can manifest our glorious destinies in Christ. We need to maintain quietness by shutting the door on ourselves, so we can access the deep things of God.

Engaging the Act of Meditation

We live in a noisy world, where everything around us constitutes a distraction. The act of meditation requires the quietness of our hearts as well as our environment. That is why when we are on the verge of making important decisions, we must seek a quiet place.

We need to carve out time to engage in meditation, separating ourselves to seek and intermeddle with wisdom from the Word (Proverbs 18:1).

In July 1999, when the Faith Tabernacle was under construction, and it seemed impossible that the Tabernacle would not be dedicated in September, I began to worship God. Then, suddenly, the Word of God came alive from Genesis chapter one.

God said to me: "I made the world in six days; I will not need two months to finish an ordinary building." That stirred up my faith, and I could boldly declare, "Two months too much!" That came from a quiet meditation.

In quietness, strength is released for exploits. Therefore, there is no substitute for quietness, both within and without, as far as meditation is concerned. Quietness enables us to search for quality answers to tackle every issue of concern. We must seek it at all cost. If our houses are too noisy, we can lodge in a hotel. We need to invest this time to achieve our desired turnaround.

What do we meditate on?

> ***O how love I thy law! It is my meditation all the day.***
>
> *Psalm 119:97*

We meditate on every Word we have received as our daily life nutrient, by eating and chewing it. The process of meditation covers reflections.

> ***And Isaac went out to meditate in the field at the eventide: and he lifted up his eyes, and saw, and, behold, the camels were coming.***
>
> *Genesis 24:63*

When it was time for Isaac to get married, he went on a journey of reflection. By spiritual reflection, we have divine fellowship with the Almighty, the Creator of all things. Our blessings come faster when we do a lot of reflections.

What is the Process of Finding?

A definite word relating to our situations can be found in the Word, through the help of the Holy Ghost. Meditation is allowing the Spirit to bring deeper meaning to our spirit-man.

> ***Arise, shine; for thy light is come, and the glory of the LORD is risen upon thee.***
>
> *Isaiah 60:1*

We have to picture the glory of God from His Word, and how to access that for our desired changes.

> ***Therefore thy gates shall be open continually; they shall not be shut day nor night; that men may bring unto thee the forces of the Gentiles, and that their kings may be brought.***
>
> *Isaiah 60:11*

Henceforth, picture all the promises in the Scriptures, and claim them by faith. Everything that has ever happened in this ministry has been delivered in pictures from the Scriptures and prophecies because God puts

His plans into pictures.

As in photography, the picture comes out first as negative, which in turn makes the real picture sure. Whatever you see from the Scriptures beginning from today, receive it in its raw state and war with it, till it becomes real. If you have seen your future from any scripture, I command you to take it now!

EIGHT

WORD DYNAMICS

So shall my word be that goeth forth out of my mouth: it shall not return unto me void, but it shall accomplish that which I please, and it shall prosper in the thing whereto I sent it.

Isaiah 55:11

The Word is God's weapon for compelling turnarounds. Every practical change of story in the Scriptures is rooted adequately in God's Word. God gave us an example from the account of creation. The world was dark, shapeless and formless when God said, "Let there be light!" This light brought a change of story. It is the entrance of God's Word that brings light, and He confirmed it by declaring His Word. When He declared the words of creation, everything turned around.

As it is written: ***Who being the brightness of his glory, and the express image of his person, and upholding all things by the word of his power, when he had by himself purged our sins, sat down on the right hand of the Majesty on high*** (Hebrews 1:3).

It is clear that God sustains the universe by the mighty power of His command, and this command is His Word. Now, this word is not just the word of men, but God's Word which is the Word of life. Just like iron materials are used for the production of iron, we are divine products, and only divine weapons can change our status in life.

We can only command the supernatural by divine command, which means, we can only take command by engaging the Word of God.

It is important to also know that the Word that guarantees a turnaround is the sent Word, the right Word and the Word in season.

The Sent Word

We must understand that for every earthly challenge, there is a heavenly solution, which is packaged in the Word. Therefore, we must trust God for the sent Word.

The Lord sent a Word to Jacob that turned him to a

generational phenomenon. He also sent a Word to Abraham, turning him to a generational figure.

The Lord sent a word into Jacob, and it hath lighted upon Israel (Isaiah 9:8).

The "sent word" is what makes stars in the Kingdom. No one ever accesses a sent word without emerging a star at the end. The word came to Gideon, "Oh thou mighty man of valour, the Lord is with you." At that point, there was nothing mighty about his generation, but the sent word made him a star.

The sent word puts us supernaturally in command. This centres on what God has "spoken", not what is "written". Abraham was celebrating his sons as many as the sand by the seashore. Nobody could see it, but the sent word opened his eyes to see it and gave him confidence.

...according to that which was spoken, So shall thy seed be (Romans 4:18).

Abraham, by the sent word, became the symbol of generational blessing. The Bible says: ***He staggered not at the promise of God through unbelief; but was strong in faith, giving glory to God; And being fully persuaded that, what he had promised, he was able also to perform*** (Romans 4:20-21).

Nothing triggers a turnaround like a sent Word because God cannot deny Himself.

As it is written: ***God is not a man, that he should lie; neither the son of man, that he should repent: hath he said, and shall he not do it? Or hath he spoken, and shall he not make it good?*** (Numbers 23:19)

Many years before we moved to Canaanland, God told me that He would build for Himself a place that would seat multitudes of people. Therefore, when He directed us to move our headquarters to Lagos and referred to Canaanland as the centre where the world would be reached, I believed Him.

When God says a thing, it is final. He means what He says, and says what He means. When God says it and we are "stupid" enough to believe it, we have committed His integrity to perform His Word.

For it is written: ***And blessed is she that believed: for there shall be a performance of those things which were told her from the Lord*** (Luke 1:45).

It is important to understand that only men of the Spirit can access the sent word. John was in the Spirit on the Island of Patmos when God revealed to him the things that were to come.

For he said: ***I was in the Spirit on the Lord's Day, and heard...*** (Revelation 1:10).

We cannot receive the Word from God concerning our situation with a carnal mind. This is because the carnal mind cannot access the things of the Spirit, because it is foolishness to him. It takes only the spiritual mind to get what God is saying and we need His Word to access our turnarounds in life.

The sent Word is called "Rhema" and it brings out the greatness in us. Most of the time, the sent Word comes with instructions that are ordained for our distinction. God said to me, "The Harvest of Africa is now overripe, rush in and preserve it from decadence," and we reached out to Africa by His grace.

Do not mistake the written word for the spoken word. Thank God for the written word, but the spoken word is one major key to our supernatural and unstoppable breakthroughs.

The Right Word

This refers to accessing the mysteries in the Word. It is the Holy Ghost-interpreted word. No one can interpret a book better than the author. The Holy Ghost is the Author of the Bible on God's behalf; holy men spoke as they were moved by the Holy Ghost. He is the Master interpreter of the truth. No one can interpret the truth better than Him.

When the Holy Ghost steps in to interpret the Word, He brings about an in-depth understanding. It was His Word, which is the right word, that provoked the turnaround that changed the world of emptiness to that of beauty.

No matter the size of darkness or emptiness around our lives, it will always bow to the authority of the right Word. The right word refers to the key that opens the breakthrough door to a particular situation. If we don't give attention to it, we may never take delivery of our turnarounds.

It is written: ***How forcible are right words...*** (Job 6:25).

It is not just the word that guarantees a turnaround, but the right word. When the Holy Ghost comes into us, He teaches us all things. He networks scriptures like technical entities and delivers an amazing product that cannot be mistaken for another.

The Holy Spirit is the Master Networker of scriptures in bringing about what we need to maximise the blessings that are contained in the Scriptures. For instance, He said to me, "Seek ye first My Kingdom and all these things that others are dying to get shall be added unto you." That is His interpretation of Matthew 6:33.

Many years ago, He also said to me: "My son, my prosperity plan is not a promise; it does not answer to prayers. It is not a promise; it has no respect for fasting. It is a covenant, and until your part is played, I am not committed." That is the Holy Ghost breaking down scriptures to consumable terms. This was in relation to His covenant in Deuteronomy 8:18.

God said, "As long as you see the sun and the moon in the sky, know that my covenant is in force." That means, this covenant remains in force while the earth remains. When the Holy Ghost interpreted this to me, I knew I had command. He broke it down in consumable terms and when I swallowed it, it turned me on.

A most graphic interpretation of that is in Job 33:21-25, which says:

> ***His flesh is consumed away, that it cannot be seen; and his bones that were not seen stick out.***
>
> ***Yea, his soul draweth near unto the grave, and his life to the destroyers.***
>
> ***If there be a messenger with him, an interpreter, one among a thousand, to shew unto man his uprightness:***
>
> ***Then he is gracious unto him, and saith, Deliver him from going down to the pit: I have found a ransom.***
>
> ***His flesh shall be fresher than a child's: he shall return to the days of his youth.***

When we encounter the right word, the intensity of the word changes everything about us.

On September 4, 1987, while at Sheraton hotel, I read from Hebrews 7:1-8. Then the Interpreter (the Holy Spirit) said, "The same way I open heaven over individuals, I also open heaven over organisations, companies and corporations, including churches." He further revealed that the tithe Abraham paid was not a personal but company tithe.

That word came to me as tonic and turned me on. I knew immediately that I had gotten the key to supernatural supplies for our Commission. I never read the interpretation from a book; God visited me and opened my eyes to the truth. That, subsequently, made the heavens open over the ministry. When we find the Holy Ghost interpreted word, it establishes our supernatural turnaround.

The Word in Season

There is a word in season that clears weariness and brings about a refreshing. It is a word sent to address our present situation and generate a divine solution. It is an "on the spot word". It addresses our specific needs at a set time.

> ***The Lord GOD hath given me the tongue of the learned, that I should know how to speak a word in season to him that is weary: he wakeneth morning by morning, he wakeneth mine ear to hear***

as the learned. The Lord GOD hath opened mine ear, and I was not rebellious, neither turned away back.

Isaiah 50:4-5

A word in season entitles us to unstoppable proofs. It terminates the fear and doubt we might have had while examining the situation. The greater our insight on the challenge at hand, the bolder we become while challenging it and the surer we are of our victory.

Then said Jesus unto them, When ye have lifted up the Son of man, then shall ye know that I am he, and that I do nothing of myself; but as my Father hath taught me, I speak these things.

John 8:28

I can of mine own self do nothing: as I hear, I judge: and my judgment is just; because I seek not mine own will, but the will of the Father which hath sent me.

John 5:30

During the attack on our last daughter by the spirit of death, I prayed saying, "Lord, there must be a way out." Then, I reached out to my drawer, brought out a piece of simple literature and the light in a scripture came forth.

What time I am afraid, I will trust in thee (Psalm 56:3).

The author of the book explained, "When fear knocks on the door, send faith to open the door and you will discover that there is no one there." Then, revelation began to flow from Revelation 1:18, "I AM He that was dead, and behold, I AM alive and I live forevermore. I have the keys of hell and of death and I am holding the keys in favour of my children." That was the end of the challenge.

The word in season is that Word from the Scripture that tackles our particular need. It is not just the Word we access that makes us a wonder, but how much of the Word we imbibe. It is how well we apply ourselves to the dictates of the revelation that matters, not the revelation we acquire.

Too many people are filled with unapplied revelations. Things are not working because they are not putting the revelations they have encountered to work. It is putting God's Word to work, believing that it will manifest, that triggers the supernatural. I pray that you will be initiated into the workings of God's sent Word, His right Word, and His Word in season in Jesus' name!

NINE

VIRTUES IN THE WORD

And the Word was made flesh, and dwelt among us, (and we beheld his glory, the glory as of the only begotten of the Father), full of grace and truth.

John 1:14

We now understand that a word from the Lord on any issue of life puts us in command of that issue. As highlighted in some previous chapters, it takes a word from the Lord to exercise authority. It is as I hear, not as I read or as they said. It is as I hear, that I determine and decide what happens, and I'm always in charge

(John 5:30).

God's Word is loaded with wonder genes, and when we are inoculated with them, we will begin to manifest the wonders that the Word carries.

The Psalmist says: ***Open thou mine eyes, that I may behold wondrous things out of thy law*** (Psalm 119:18).

When you take a glass of water and ask a layman, "What is in that cup?" He will say, "It is water." However, when you ask a chemistry student, he will likely tell you that it is a compound of hydrogen and oxygen in some percentages. That is because he has been given access to the knowledge of the chemical content of that colourless liquid. That is what the Word of God is like; it is loaded with some stuff and when the Holy Ghost leads us into them, we begin to experience the effect of those things in our lives.

The Word of God has life; that means, it is made up of genes, which energise the living capacity of the Word. We will examine the different genetic components of the Word below.

The Virtues in the Word

Jesus said: ***Somebody touched me: for I perceived virtue is gone out of me*** (Luke 8:46).

"Virtue", here, means power and we are empowered

by the Word of God. Jesus was preaching and the power of God was present to heal all that were oppressed and battered by the devil. Thus, virtue is equal to God's healing power (Luke 5:17).

Jesus said, "The Scripture cannot be broken." The Scripture is loaded with life and death; therefore, it brings certain things to pass. We cannot pray against them, but we can exempt some things from happening. A picture of what God has ordained to happen in our time has been revealed in the Bible.

The Word is Genetically Illuminative

The Word has power to illuminate us and this empowers us to dominate darkness. When Jesus came, evil spirits fled at His appearance, because He carried light. Nothing threatens darkness like light.

> ***In the beginning was the Word, and the Word was with God, and the Word was God.***
>
> ***The same was in the beginning with God.***
>
> ***All things were made by him; and without him was not anything made that was made.***
>
> ***In him was life; and the life was the light of men.***
>
> ***That was the true Light, which lighteth every man that cometh into the world.***
>
> *John 1:1-4, 9*

The Word does not only enlighten us, but we are lighted by it. The Word of God is supernaturally illuminative. It has the capacity to illuminate us with divine light, so we can dominate every realm of darkness. When we are thoroughly illuminated, every foul force recognises it.

When we travelled to Liberia years ago, "the Queen of Sheba", who is known as an infamous follower of Lucifer and has practiced satanism for years, was lodged in the same hotel as I was. When we arrived at the hotel, she could not stay. She left unceremoniously, because light descended there. Therefore, to excel in this Kingdom, we need light!

"Devils" know light bearers. You can pretend in church, but you cannot pretend when it comes to taking command because the entrance of God's Word gives light! (Psalm 119:130).

We are programmed and ordained for a turnaround adventure on earth. For anyone challenged, turnaround is your right and for anyone on the highway of life, turnaround is your heritage.

We are expected to crave a change of level, spiritually, socially, in our business, career, with our children and family. This is because there is nothing small that cannot become big and there is nothing big that cannot become bigger.

Thank God for your great job, but what if God had ordained you to be a great employer of labour? Thank God for the business you started and the few people working for you, but what if that is not what God has ordained for you? What if you are supposed to have 500,000 people working in your organisation?

When we came into Canaanland, I had rest within me because I thought we would have just one service. Suddenly, we commenced the second, third, fourth, and now, we hold five services and we are still moving on. All because God said so!

As it is written: ***Thou shalt be blessed above all people: there shall not be male or female barren among you, or among your cattle*** (Deuteronomy 7:14).

We are a people of equal destiny but it is understanding that differentiates one from another. If you can catch a word from the Lord, no matter how many devils are behind your issues, you will be supernaturally successful. Until we stop doing what changes our level, our turnarounds cannot stop. Anything we do with understanding produces outstanding results. We can only stop what challenges our turnarounds, by speaking the Word pertaining to that situation.

On September 7, 1983, the Lord said to me, "My son, you have two eyes. Can you make one look up and the other look down?" Then He explained, "Any time you are looking unto man, never claim to be looking unto Me because they looked unto Me and they were lightened and their faces were no longer ashamed" (Psalm 34:5).

From that day, I looked away from myself. That is applying the Word received from God to give you an instant turnaround. This can be explained as accessing the light of the Word.

God's Word is Genetic

...the words that I speak unto you, they are spirit, and they are life (John 6:63).

God's Word contains life-quickening genes. Anything living has genes within it. Thus, God's Word has life genes.

> ***And the Word was made flesh, and dwelt among us, (and we beheld his glory, the glory as of the only begotten of the Father,) full of grace and truth.***
>
> *John 1:14*

The Word was made flesh. This goes further to establish the fact that God's Word carries genes within It. So, God's Word is genetic, with the ability to transform the life of anyone that encounters It.

These spiritual genes can also bring about a spiritual re-engineering of our destinies. A gene is a part of a cell in a living thing, which controls its physical characteristics, growth and development. God's Word is able to penetrate our bone marrows and reconfigure it.

This is why, by God's Word and anointing, a rotten kidney can be restored and a terminal phase of life can be reversed. We have heard several testimonies of how cancer was destroyed and messed up by the reception of God's Word.

As it is written: ***For the word of God is quick, and powerful, and sharper than any twoedged sword, piercing even to the dividing asunder of soul and spirit, and of the joints and marrow, and is a discerner of the thoughts and intents of the heart*** (Hebrews 4:12).

In 1983, someone who had blood in his faeces and was booked for surgery attended one of our programmes. During the Word, he said he felt a touch on his body, and went to the restroom. For the first time in six years, he defecated without blood in his faeces. The power in the Word instantly healed him.

God's Word is Creative

When a word from the Lord comes, it creates even what is not in existence. When God said, "Let there be light," there was light. Everything God said, He saw. God's Word is genetically creative; it can create brand new organs for the body. Whatever is not curable must be repairable and whatever is not repairable, must be replaceable.

In 1983, I met a woman in Jos. She and her husband had been looking for the fruit of the womb for years. They had gone everywhere, even done In Vitro Fertilization (IVF), and the doctors confirmed she had no womb. The Word of the Lord came to me that:

> ***The thief cometh not, but for to steal, and to kill, and to destroy: I am come that they might have life, and that they may have it more abundantly.***
>
> *John 10:10*

Jesus came to replace in the most perfect form whatever the thief had stolen. So, I said to her, "The devil stole that womb and if you believe Jesus, He would replace it with a new one." Her faith grew, and that was the end of the issue. Nine months later, she delivered a bouncing baby boy.

Whatever the devil has stolen is replaceable in God's genetically creative Word.

Jesus said to Mary, "Thy brother shall live again." As the word went forth, the creative forces of the word penetrated the grave, all the decomposed organs were replaced and fresh blood began to flow in the vein. Even after four days, under the heat of the tomb, Lazarus that was dead came forth. That is a demonstration of the creative power of the Word (John 11:23-44).

God's Word is not a motivational factor. No! It is far beyond it. There is no motivational technology that can generate what this ministry experiences today. It can only be by the force of God's Word.

Years ago, a little child died in our church in Abuja. That night, I had a brief meeting with them and as I stood on the platform and said, "Is there no balm in Gilead?" The arrows in the creative genes of the Word went through to the third floor of the children's department, where the child was kept, and life surged into the child that was certified dead since about 1:30 p.m.

We do not need to add anything to God to live healthy. He said, ***I am the Lord that healeth thee.*** I am the Lord, I am more than enough for your health needs. I am Jehovah Rapha, there is no one else next to Me (Exodus 15:26).

Every Word from the Lord creates our desires. If any part of the body proves incurable, it must be repairable; if it is not repairable, it must of necessity be replaceable. Thus, God's Word can replace any damaged part of our bodies.

We must understand that God's Word can come through rhema, which is the voice behind the statement of the Scriptures, or through the ministry of the prophets.

God's Word is Prophetic

Every word from the Scriptures is prophetic, which means that it has an assurance of delivery. This is called the more sure Word of prophecy. When God's Word of prophecy comes, its fulfilment is guaranteed (2 Peter 1:21-22).

God said: ***So shall my word be that goeth forth out of my mouth: it shall not return unto me void, but it shall accomplish that which I please, and it shall prosper in the thing whereto I sent it*** (Isaiah 55:11).

When God says a thing, His integrity backs it up. Any Word spoken by God to you is ordained for fulfilment because it is prophetic in nature, except you do not believe it.

However, we must understand that we have the responsibility to war with it until the day dawns and the daystar rises in our hearts.

Most people think God's Word is just principles, but our constant search gives us more than that. In 1996, I read from John 5:26, and discovered that "as the Father has light in Himself, so has He given to the Son to have light in Himself and the Son can quicken whosoever He will." God's Word is prophetic and when we believe it, we have committed God to perform it – whether He speaks to us directly, or by the revealed Word.

When the Lord spoke to me in response to who pays me in my ministerial work, He took me through the Scriptures by the Holy Ghost. I saw a very large package as my benefit for serving Him; it was too much. This is because I had already seen my future and what is lined up for me in the Word. We cannot see a future and still be downcast. Whatever word we have found, is a pointer to the glorious future that awaits us. This is because revelation puts us in command of the future.

I have seen my future, and only rapture can terminate it. Many years ago, I told a congregation, "All that you will earn till you die, without eating from it, cannot run this ministry for one year." It is a harsh statement, but I used it because I found the source. Whatever God speaks to us today is awaiting delivery tomorrow, if we will believe it now.

We need to become that Bartimaeus who would not let Jesus pass without dropping his own blessing. Become that Jacob who would not let the angel go until you are blessed with a change of name.

When Jesus told Simon to cast his net into the deep in the book of Luke chapter 5 from verse 1-7, He created all the fishes they caught. Simon did not need to do anything; He brought everything they needed into the net. There is something we desperately need that must be created, and this can only be by the revelation of the Word.

God's Word is an Indestructible Seed

Now the parable is this: The seed is the Word of God (Luke 8:11).

It is also written: ***So shall my word that goeth forth out of my mouth: it shall not return unto me void, but it shall accomplish that which I please, and it shall prosper in the things whereto I sent it*** (Isaiah 55:11; see also Matthew 24:35).

It takes the Word from God for anyone to truly take command of any issue of life. You need a Word from the Lord, not "a word of God". A word sent to you!

Concerning Joseph, the Bible says: ***Until the time that His word came, the word of the LORD tried Him.*** But when his word came ***the king sent and loosed him; even the ruler of the people, and let him go free*** (Psalm 105:19-20), and turned his story around dramatically. It took just one day to transform Joseph, and it came by the Word.

Until his word came, the struggles continued; but when his word came, his turnaround occurred. Our turnarounds are only guaranteed by the Word from the Lord. We have reduced God's Word to mere humanistic principles. Everyone is shouting about what they cannot experience. God's Word must surely produce because His integrity is at stake.

Longevity Genes

The last enemy slated for destruction is called death. As it is written: ***The last enemy that shall be destroyed is death*** (I Corinthians 15:26). God has ordained that death must lose its destructive power in the church.

In 1983, on a Friday night, I taught a series on "Power over Death". The teachings were transformational and impactful; I knew I heard from God that satan had lost all power. All power in heaven and on earth has been given to God, and when we remove all, what is remaining? Nothing! So, whatever the devil may claim to have is fake. On Saturday, I had an encounter with death as the devil came to try that Word. While on the verge of death, the voice in my spirit spoke out, "What are you doing here?" And my spirit responded, "I don't know too!" With that force, I jerked off from the deathbed and dashed into the bathroom to shower. I travelled that same day, enthusiastic to "meet" death on the way and "kill" it.

The Bible says concerning Jesus that His detractors could not kill Him because His hour had not yet come.

> ***Then they sought to take him: but no man laid hands on him, because his hour was not yet come.***
>
> *John 7:30*

Everyone has an appointed time with God. Therefore, the devil is not permitted to cut short our destinies because God has ordained specific number of years for each one of us and we can only get that by the revelation of the Word.

It is written: ***And the LORD said, my spirit shall not always strive with man, for that he also is flesh: yet his days shall be an hundred and twenty years*** (Genesis 6:3).

Life and death are by choice. God said, "...I have set before you life and death, blessing and cursing: therefore choose life..." (Deuteronomy 30:19). We have longevity genes in the Word. For instance, Moses heard from the Lord in Genesis 6:3, and in Deuteronomy chapter 34 verse 7, he was one hundred and twenty years old and his eyes were not dim. He was strong and agile. Anything we hear from God stands forever. I have heard from the Lord and I am excited about life. I will be on earth for a very long time because I have seen myself ministering in the year 2035.

One day, I was in a vision where I saw myself standing by the Communion table at an extreme old age. What the Holy Spirit does is to turn the Scriptures to pictures. Friend, death shall not have access to your life, in the name of Jesus!

God's Word is Medicinal

He sent his word, and healed them, and delivered them from their destructions.

Psalm 107:20

There are healing virtues in the Word, because there is a healing God in it, and His Word carries the same order of healing virtue in Him. Therefore, God's Word is not just genetic; it is also medicinal. By medicinal, I mean, it contains therapeutic values. His Word brings healing to our spirit, soul and body.

The centurion answered and said, Lord, I am not worthy that thou shouldest come under my roof: but speak the word only, and my servant shall be healed.

Matthew 8:8

As soon as Jesus spoke the Word, the therapeutic virtues in the Word brought about the healing of the Centurion's servant. Thus, when we drink the Word daily, it transfers life genes, and healing virtues flow through us (John 6:63).

My son, attend to my words; incline thine ear unto my sayings. Let them not depart from thine eyes; keep them in the midst of thine heart. For they are life unto those that find them, and health to all their flesh.

Proverbs 4:20-22

When the healing Word fills our hearts and minds, it manifests naturally through spoken words; and when it rules our spirit, thoughts and life, we live healthy. The Word rules and keeps our spirit-man alive, thereby making us unbreakable.

We need to let the Word take root in our spirit to keep us confidently in command of any situation that poses as a challenge to us. This can be achieved when our hearts are focused on the finished work of Christ in our lives.

We cannot tap into the healing virtue of God until it is rooted in our minds and spirit. If our minds are overwhelmed by the truth, we are in control. We need to have an understanding of what the Word carries, and recognise that our total health is part of the virtues in the Word.

God's Word is Surgical

It has the capacity to create our desired solutions. Examining the woman that was bent over in Luke 13:11-13, Jesus performed instant surgery on her and she was made straight that same hour. All He said was, "Woman, thou art loosed from thine infirmity." That brought about instant healing.

> ***For the word of God is quick, and powerful, and sharper than any twoedged sword, piercing even to***

the dividing asunder of soul and spirit, and of the joints and marrow, and is a discerner of the thoughts and intents of the heart.

Hebrews 4:12

Every time we approach God for His Word, we must understand that His Word carries all we need for our health and life. By His Word, He created a tooth for someone during a service. He does what has never been heard of historically.

When God made man, He said that it was not good for man to be alone; so He made a helpmeet for him. God caused a great sleep to come upon Adam in Genesis 2:21-22. Then, He opened up his flesh and removed a rib, with which He made a woman. That is surgery!

God performed an overnight surgery on the man called Adam and from him, He brought forth a woman called Eve. And He said: ***For I am the Lord, I change not...*** (Malachi 3:6).

The Bible says: ***In the beginning was the word, and the word was with God and the word was God*** (John 1:1).

Since God is the Master Surgeon, His Word is also surgical in nature. It took God four days to create the fullness of the world; it took Him only one day to make man. Therefore, it will not take Him more than a day to repair or replace whatever is damaged in our lives.

TEN

COVENANT OF SCRIPTURES

All Scripture is given by inspiration of God, and is profitable for doctrine, for reproof, for correction, for instruction in righteousness; that the man of God may be perfect, throughly furnished unto all good works.

2 Timothy 3:16-17

The Bible is a book of covenants and that is why we have the Old and New Testaments which also mean Old and New Covenants. "Covenant" means there is always what we must do to draw on the finished work of Christ. Jesus already paid the price with His Blood, which is all we need to live life at its best. However, to draw on it, there are demands that should be kept.

The reason people remain in captivity, despite the profitable provisions God has reserved for them, is that most Christians are afraid of taking responsibility. We serve a covenant-keeping God, Who has left for us a Book of covenants for anyone who is interested in any of His provisions. The plans to be met are clearly enumerated in the book of covenants, but we have to search, find, and apply them so they can work for us.

> ***And the vision of all is become unto you as the words of a book that is sealed, which men deliver to one that is learned, saying, Read this, I pray thee: and he saith, I cannot; for it is sealed: And the book is delivered to him that is not learned, saying, Read this, I pray thee: and he saith, I am not learned.***
>
> *Isaiah 29:11-12*

A covenant is not a mysterious or mystical statement that cannot be decoded; it is committing to the conditions of a promise. All scriptures are given for our profiting and if we give ourselves wholly to what God says, He will make our profiting appear to all. To every promise of the Scriptures, there are conditions and when these conditions are met, the promise graduates into a covenant, committing God's integrity to perform, because He cannot deny Himself (1 Timothy 4:15).

God is always mindful of His covenant. Years ago, I saw from the Scriptures that if I am delighted in obeying God's voice, He will project His goodness in my life to my generation. This is because He said: ***...the generation of the upright shall be blessed. Wealth and***

riches shall be in his house... (Psalm 112:2-3).

A covenant is a deal enacted by God based on well-defined terms and sealed with an oath. The deal is contained in the book of deals called, the Bible.

God covenanted with mankind on the sustainability of the earth. He said, "While the earth remaineth, seedtime and harvest... shall not cease" (Genesis 8:22). Just like day and night, and summer and winter, seed time and harvest will be there. That means multiplication will be sequel to seed time. Nothing multiplies without something sown.

That is, this earth will never lack fruit but the fruit of the earth will only answer to the covenant of seed time and harvest. This confirms what God said to me in March 1982, that: "Prosperity does not answer to prayers and it has no respect for fasting, it only answers to covenant practice. Until your part is played, I am not committed to My part."

One of the conditions for having our diverse needs met is Kingdom service or stewardship. Remember:

> ***And ye shall serve the Lord your God, and he shall bless thy bread, and thy water; and I will take sickness away from the midst of thee. There shall nothing cast their young, nor be barren, in thy land: the number of thy days I will fulfil.***
>
> *Exodus 23:25-26*

God wants to bless us but we must serve Him to get

His blessings. You shall serve and God shall bless. You shall serve and you shall not be barren. You shall serve and you shall not suffer miscarriage; you shall serve and He will take sickness away from you. There is what we must do before we can access what God has provided for us.

This is what makes Christianity a covenant-based faith, because we serve a covenant making and keeping God.

He said: ***My covenant will I not break, nor alter the thing that is gone out of my lips*** (Psalm 89:34).

We are only empowered to access and take delivery of our inheritances on the platform of the covenant.

> ***But thou shalt remember the Lord thy God: for it is he that giveth thee power to get wealth, that he may establish his covenant which he sware unto thy fathers, as it is this day.***
>
> *Deuteronomy 8:18*

Therefore, God empowers us to access the provisions He has made as we operate by the covenant.

Christianity is a faith, based on shared responsibility. I once said in one of the teachings on faith that, "Any faith that seeks to make God absolutely responsible for the outcome of our lives is an irresponsible faith." We have a share of the responsibility in order to have our inheritances delivered. Other covenants that guarantee our turnaround in all areas of need are:

Covenant of Health

Life at its best will be theoretical without health. Just as doctors have their prescription for certain illnesses, God also has His prescriptions for our total health and the price has been fully paid.

> ***For ye are bought with a price: therefore glorify God in your body, and in your spirit, which are God's.***
>
> *1 Corinthians 6:20*

God has a full healthcare package for His children. He said: "Beloved, I wish above all things that thou mayest prosper and be in health, even as thy soul prospereth" (3 John 2). Our total health is very important to God and health is the only way to validate abundant life.

The price has been paid for a sickness and disease-free life. He said, by His stripes we were healed. This implies that our healing was settled from the beginning (Isaiah 53:5; I Peter 2:24).

God's Word carries God's nature and is immune to sicknesses and diseases. When we receive and believe the Word, we buy into the divine nature that establishes our dominion over every assault on our bodies.

But He said: ***My son, attend to my words; incline thine ear unto my sayings. Let them not depart from thine eyes; keep them in the midst of thine heart. For they are life unto those that find them, and health to all their flesh*** (Proverbs 4:20-22).

This implies that all our inheritances in Christ are locked up in the Scriptures, and healing is one of those redemptive heritages in Christ. He took our infirmities and bore our sicknesses. Therefore, when we receive the Word concerning our inheritance of divine health, the healing power of God is released to make us whole.

As it is written: ***Whereby are given unto us exceeding great and precious promises: that by these ye might be partakers of the divine nature, having escaped the corruption that is in the world through lust*** (2 Peter 1:4).

These exceeding great and precious promises are not only to be claimed, they impart divine nature into our lives. When we receive and believe the Word, divine nature is imparted and by that, we dominate every assault on our body and soul. Thus, we partake of divine nature from the Word, which means dominion over sicknesses and diseases.

Covenant of Favour

Nothing beautifies destiny like favour. The beauty of the destinies of Daniel, Shadrach, Meshach and Abednego came on the platform of favour that the Lord gave them.

Joseph enjoyed favour in slavery and in the prison; and favour took him finally to the palace. Favour is one of the returns that we are entitled to when we seek

God's Kingdom first.

The Bible says: ***Thou shalt arise, and have mercy upon Zion: for the time to favour her, yea, the set time, is come. For thy servants take pleasure in her stones, and favour the dust thereof. So the heathen shall fear the name of the Lord, and all the kings of the earth thy glory*** (Psalm 102:13-15).

Therefore, His favour brings us glory and beauty. For instance, the Bible says: ***Whoso findeth a wife findeth a good thing, and obtaineth favour of the Lord*** (Proverbs 18:22).

Therefore, one of the manifestations of favour is miracle marriage. Also, note that you cannot have favour with your husband and end up separated. You cannot have favour with your wife and she walks out on you. Favour makes marriage harmonious and beautiful.

Furthermore, favour breaks the yoke of marital spells, because marriage is a good thing and was ordained by God. He said, "It is not good for a man to be alone." So, marriage is a good thing created by God for man to fulfil destiny in a grand style.

The Covenant of Prosperity

Every child of God is a seed of Abraham and is ordained to be an heir of the blessings upon Abraham. Therefore, God is still in the business of turning people into financial giants because according to the Bible, we have access in Christ, to whatever God said to Abraham. As it is written:

> ***And if ye be Christ's, then are ye Abraham's seed, and heirs according to the promise.***
>
> *Galatians 3:29*

God's prosperity plan has no respect for prayer because it is a covenant and not a promise. It is the revelation of the covenant of prosperity from the Scriptures that puts us in command of financial fortune. This is because God's Word is the highway to our inheritances and we must be committed to finding what it takes to access it. For instance, there are several covenant demands we must fulfil for our prosperity to materialise.

The anchor law of the covenant of prosperity is giving. This is because only givers qualify for God's blessings. According to the Scriptures, it is the giving law that launches men into realms of financial fortune because our seeds entitle us to harvests (Genesis 8:22; Job 22:21-27).

Therefore, giving is the gateway to supernatural supplies. As it is written: ***He hath dispersed, he hath given to the poor; his righteousness endureth for ever; his horn shall be exalted with honour*** (Psalm 112:9). He brought wealth into his house by dispersing his resources and giving to the poor. That's why his generation is blessed.

When we give to the point that the law becomes operational in our lives, according to scriptural principles, it launches us into realms of financial fortune.

It is not the Word we find that matters but what we do with it. We discover from the Scriptures that every divine supply answers to man's obedience. Mary said, "Whatsoever He saith unto you, do it" (John 2:5). They were to pay taxes in Matthew chapter 17 verse 27, and Jesus told Peter to go to the sea, cast a hook and open the mouth of the first fish he would catch to get the money required to pay the tax collector.

Now, think of what Job the wealthiest man of his time said, "As I was in the days of my youth, when the secret of God was upon my tabernacle..." What was that secret? He was eyes to the blind and feet to the lame. The cause that he knew not, he searched out. That was the secret behind the wealth and the supplies that Job enjoyed (Job 29:2-18).

It was not his business expertise that brought him to that level of honour; it was his covenant practice. The secret to divine supplies is rooted in giving. Job got the secret of God, traded with it, and became the wealthiest man in his time. The Bible says he became the greatest of all men in the East (Job 1:1-5).

Also, there is the law of tithing, which is the gateway to a world of financial fortune. It is God's commandment that opens the windows of heaven to us, for the showers of God's blessings. The following scriptures establish the place of tithe:

> ***And all the tithe of the land, whether of the seed of the land, or of the fruit of the tree, is the Lord's: it is holy unto the Lord.***
>
> *Leviticus 27:30*

The Bible further states:

> ***Thou shalt truly tithe all the increase of thy seed, that the field bringeth forth year by year.***
>
> *Deuteronomy 14:22*

Tithe is the tenth of our increase or income. It is the covenant acknowledgement of God's blessings in our lives that entitles us to a continuous flow of such blessings. It is also God's portion that makes the remainder meaningful. When we stop tithing, we stop the flow of God's blessings in our lives (Malachi 3:10).

This is why we must understand that tithing is not a church doctrine; it is a covenant of the Kingdom that launches the believer into realms of financial prosperity. Therefore, tithing is a Kingdom mystery that confers us with mastery over our finances. It is a covenant obligation for everyone who desires to step into his wealthy place in Christ.

ELEVEN

ENGAGING THE WORD

Thy words were found, and I did eat them; and thy word was unto me the joy and rejoicing of mine heart: for I am called by thy name, O LORD God of hosts.

Jeremiah 15:16

Light is our guarantee for a turnaround. Our turnarounds do not answer to stories; they answer to mysteries. Turnaround only answers to the efficacy of light; it has nothing to do with age. We can be as old as Methuselah in the church; if we lack light, we will lack testimonies.

It is light that empowers us for dominion, not letters.

Therefore, we need to remain spiritual to receive light, or we will be running around with letters, mistaking it for light.

An understanding of the Word makes us supernaturally fruitful. We cannot lack proofs in our lives when we understand the Word. It is spiritual understanding that we call light. When we are not spiritual, we disqualify ourselves because it is what gives us access to the mysteries of the Kingdom. By it, we gain mastery over the issues of life. Anybody can access the letters; only the spiritual can access the light.

Apostle Paul said in Ephesians 5:14: ***Wherefore he saith, Awake thou that sleepest, and arise from the dead, and Christ shall give thee light***.

Access to light requires that we awake from our slumber as casual Christians. We have to arise to take responsibility, or we will never encounter light, and our situations will remain the same. We know that the devil takes advantage of us when we are asleep to gain control over our lives. Therefore, we need to be awake to safeguard every aspect of our lives.

Jesus said: "...while men slept, his enemy came and sowed tares..." (Matthew 13:25). There are people who are sleeping with their troubles, and they have done nothing about it. This is because they have not taken responsibility to labour and engage the Word to deliver their desires.

It is light that turns a little man into a thousand and a small one to a strong nation. Light births a nation out of a person; but light does not just come, people go for light. Only those who arise to its demands, access the light (Isaiah 60:1, 8, 22).

Access to light also demands a desperate thirst. Hence, we must make gaining light our major priority, a necessary project and a "do or die" affair. In Luke 10:42, Jesus said, ***But one thing is needful***. Our principal need is to access the Word that puts us in command, because when that Word comes, our command becomes unquestionable.

We must also understand that the Holy Ghost shall teach us all things. He shall teach us vocations and skills, and how to enjoy our divine turnarounds. He will also bring all things to our remembrance, which are spoken of us by God.

He is the divine "Illuminator". He opens a man's eyes to see beyond the letters. He is the One Who shows us how to connect to our turnaround light switches. Every light has a switch but the Holy Ghost is the Custodian of that switch. He shows us how to press the switch that will make our light shine.

Influence of Light over Darkness

> ***The entrance of thy words giveth light; it giveth understanding unto the simple.***
>
> *Psalm 119:130*

> ***And the light shineth in darkness; and the darkness comprehended it not.***
>
> *John 1:5*

The strength of darkness is the absence of light. Darkness poses as something so great when light is not present. Whenever light shows up, darkness leaves. There is no negotiation.

Similarly, the glory of light is in the presence of darkness. You will agree with me that when we are in our houses during the day, we will have no need to switch on the light. No matter how much it costs us to buy those fittings, we will not need to switch them on during the day, because there is enough light from the sun.

However, when it gets dark, we will have no option but to put on the light. This is why I said that the glory of light is in the presence of darkness. Nothing puts us in command over the forces of darkness like the light that we bear.

Every light-bearer is an anointed and stress-free commander over darkness, because darkness is helpless wherever there is light. If there is one thing that we must desperately do, it is to possess this light.

We do not have any special problem; we are only victims of special ignorance, which is caused by our lack of knowledge and application of the Word. What we do with the Word we receive, determines our glorious outcome. As we begin to apply the spoken Word of God, I see whatever that has no shape in our lives taking shape in the name of Jesus!

It is written: ***Wisdom is the principal thing; therefore get wisdom: and with all thy getting get understanding*** (Proverbs 4:7).

It is the understanding behind the application of the Word that makes it work. That is, we don't just apply the Word, but we apply it with understanding. God rose up to the challenge by engaging the vital force of the Word to turn darkness to light, to give shape to formlessness, and to change emptiness to fullness of blessings.

God's Word is the precious seed; hold on to it! In fact, even when it seems like it is not working, it will definitely produce because it is an indestructible and incorruptible seed, which preserves destiny.

Being born again, not of corruptible seed, but of incorruptible, by the word of God, which liveth and abideth for ever (1 Peter 1:23).

The Word is what we need to combat the circumstances of life. Most trials of life demand our individual responsibilities. In times of trials, it is the Word that we have received and processed that serves as our armour of light to dispel the darkness of the world.

Engage the Sword of Your Mouth

We understand that God has given us both the wisdom (the Word) and the mouth to enforce our turnaround.

> ***For I will give you a mouth and wisdom, which all your adversaries shall not be able to gainsay nor resist.***
>
> *Luke 21:15*

The Word is impotent in the lives of many because they cannot engage it for their desired change. Our mouth is our sword. It is the cooperation between our mouth and His Word that delivers the victory. This is because death and life are in the power of the tongue (Proverbs 18:21).

The Word is God's wisdom for our desired turnaround, because He upholds all things, by the Word of His power. That means, He controls all things through His Word. When we receive the Word and believe it, we are empowered supernaturally to become what the Word says (Hebrews 1:3).

The absence of God's Word makes us frustrated; but when we have access to it, we need to take command by enforcing it through our spoken words. That gives us authority over life itself. Therefore, it is engaging the Word that qualifies us for a turnaround.

We have learnt about the wonders in the Word and how to access the Word. We have also received some revelations from the Word and meditated on them. It is time to engage what we have received, in order to control the situations around us. Remember, a closed mouth is a closed destiny.

Engaging the Word means putting the Word to practice. That is, warring with every word we have received until our desired change is seen. Therefore, the Word is impotent without our engagement.

Apostle Paul encouraged Timothy in his letter to him by saying: ***This charge I commit unto thee, son Timothy, according to the prophecies which went before on thee, that thou by them mightest war a good warfare*** (1 Timothy 1:18).

Every statement of the Scripture is Spirit-born, because like begets like. When we engage the Word, we are engaging the Spirit of God as a standard against the attacks of the enemy. The Spirit of God is our guarantee for victory in every spiritual conflict.

Remember, when the devil tempted Jesus after His

40-day fast, He tackled him with "It is written," and the devil left Him. Everything standing against our glorious destinies must give way according to our declarations.

God's Word is a demonstration of His raw power. It is the light that conquers darkness and is encountered from the Word. We also encounter the Spirit of God because the Word of God is the sword of the Spirit.

> ***And take the helmet of salvation, and the sword of the Spirit, which is the word of God:***
>
> *Ephesians 6:17*

We cannot engage the Sword of the Lord and still be grounded. When we engage the Spirit of the Word against the operations of hell, we are sure of victory. When we are challenged, it is the abundance of the Word in us that speaks forth.

We don't build strength in the day of battle; we build strength ahead of the day of battle. Most of our battles don't give us the opportunity to get set; we either live ready or we become victims. This is why we must remain Word-loaded. When we are loaded with the Word, we will think the Word, speak the Word and in turn, find ourselves acting the Word.

Our lives are ultimately products of the Words we speak. Every genuine encounter with the Word, therefore, empowers us to act on it in our favour.

Some years ago, I got so enraged by one little daughter in the family who claimed to be behind the torture and torment of her father and mother. I already knew my authority over the powers of darkness, so I wanted us to have a plain field. One night, I drove her to the bush with one of my associates. When we got there, I ordered her to obey whatever I instructed and she did. When I asked her why the devil couldn't come to help her, she said, "As long as you are here, he cannot come." If we can see that we have been repositioned, we will stop being tormented and take authority by our words and actions. It is one thing to receive the Word and yet another to believe it. A combination of the two is what empowers us for dominion.

As it is written: ***But as many as received him, to them gave he power to become the sons of God, even to them that believe on his name*** (John 1:12).

What we hear is powerless until we believe it, and what we receive is helpless until we behave it. It is a combination of receiving and believing that empowers our full-scale manifestation. Therefore, it is not enough to receive the Word; we must go a little further to believe it in order to dominate our circumstances.

The revelation of the Word concerning our healing and deliverances will not deliver any more than in response to the words of our mouths. What we are loaded with only becomes effectual as we declare it in faith. We are free to declare to ourselves the things that must be and the things that should not be. We are ordained to engage our tongues to establish our dominion over the circumstances of life. Thus, everything lies in our tongues. It is what we say that we are permitted to see.

Whatever is too big for our mouths to say, will be too big for our hands to handle. It is all a battle of words, but out of the abundance of the heart the mouth speaks. When we load our hearts with the truth, the things inside us jump out naturally, because the things we say define the things we see (Matthew 12:34).

What we say today is a seed for our tomorrow. How dare you say that you cannot be sick? This is because we believe the One Who said He took our infirmities, actually did. If He took, then we cannot have it. We can actually say, we can never be poor because if we believe the One Who said our seed commits Him to our harvest, then poverty gives way in our lives.

When we declare a word concerning our situations, we should refuse to doubt it in our hearts because that is how our healings and deliverances come. Our inheritances will be delivered through our tongues. What we desire cannot be handed over to us, until it comes out of our mouths, because our mouths must say it before our hands can handle it.

It is written: ***I am the LORD thy God, which brought thee out of the land of Egypt: open thy mouth wide, and I will fill it. But my people would not hearken to my voice; and Israel would none of me. So I gave them up unto their own hearts' lust: and they walked in their own counsels. Oh that my people had hearkened unto me, and Israel had walked in my ways! I should soon have subdued their enemies, and turned my hand against their adversaries*** (Psalm 81:10-14).

Even the Almighty Himself was faced with a challenge at the beginning. The whole world was dark, empty and shapeless. He needed an instrument to make a brand new world, and that instrument was the Word.

> ***In the beginning God created the Heaven and the earth. And the earth was without form, and void; and darkness was upon the face of the deep. And the Spirit of God moved upon the face of the waters. And God said, Let there be light: and there was light.***
>
> *Genesis 1:1-3*

God engaged the spoken word to create a brand new world. That is why the Bible says in the book of Hebrews 11:3 that: ***Through faith we understand that the worlds were framed by the word of God...***

At a time, David had the privilege to face Goliath, who had been a terror to the Israelites. When Saul gave him his armour to fight the battle, it was a weight; he had never proved it. The Word we have not proved cannot give us proofs! The Word we have not processed cannot process our miracles! David left what he had not proved and took what he had proved. Just a shot of what he had proved brought down the head of Goliath. Therefore, we need a proven Word to bring down every "Goliath" that is against our turnarounds.

The intensity of the light we encounter from the Word determines the level of command we exercise. You are long overdue for a change of level; your own package will not be lost to carelessness, carnality and procrastination!

In December 1983, I received a Word from the Lord that, ***In Him was life, and the life was the light of men. And the light shineth in darkness; and the darkness comprehended it not*** (John 1:4-5).

Immediately, I saw myself as a spiritual illuminant because any time we receive the Word, it illuminates our personalities and when we get into an environment, we lighten it.

The Word of God is not ordinary. It is the Word of the King and wherever the Word of the King goes, there is power. When we receive and believe God's Word, we are empowered to manifest it. It is not just power, but the power of the Almighty God that no other power can challenge (Ecclesiastes 8:4).

When we determine to walk in that light, it becomes our turn for a turnaround. It is not our turn until we decide to take responsibility for what guarantees a turnaround.

It is important to note that God's Word is impotent until we engage our own sword, which is our tongue. The Word is impotent in the lives of many because they only engage the sword of the Lord not their own sword. Our mouth is our sword. It is the cooperation between our mouths and His sword that delivers our victory. Remember, death and life are in the power of the tongue.

It is not the conflict that determines the victory but we; because we shall have whatsoever we say. The sword of the Lord will always deliver, but not without the collaboration of our sword (Mark 11:23).

We need to engage our sword to make the sword of the Lord effectual. This is because every manifestation we experience is a function of the engagement of the sword of the Lord and our sword.

For with the heart man believeth unto righteousness; and with the mouth confession is made unto salvation.

Romans 10:10

If we don't mind what we say, we will just be battered because of the misalignment of our tongue. More often than not, what we believe in our hearts does not entitle us to manifestation; it is when we declare it without shame that our profiting will be seen by all.

TWELVE

FAITH IN THE WORD

...but the word preached did not profit them, not being mixed with faith in them that heard it.

Hebrews 4:2

At the root of all divine interventions, rewards and blessings is faith because it is a determining force for God's intervention on our behalf. In tertiary institutions, there are core and elective courses; until you pass the core course, you will not be promoted to the next level.

In the same vein, faith is not an elective course in the Kingdom; it is the principal thing. Whosoever wants to see God at work in his favour, must believe that God is Who He says He is, and will do what He says He will do.

Every promise in the Bible is for our desired turnarounds, but it will only work by faith. As it is written: ***And Blessed is she that believed for there shall be a performance of those things which were told her from the Lord*** (Luke 1:45).

Faith does not just believe that God exists; it is obedience to the Word to prove that we believe Him, and that commits God to perform our desired expectations.

Our faith in the Word is fake if it is void of obedience. This is because obedience of Scripture is what gives credibility to faith. The Bible says that faith without works is dead. That means our faith is ineffective without the appropriate actions (James 2:17).

We must note that God speaks according to His strength and that strength is what triggers exploits. When His strength is engaged, it means no gate can be shut against us. His strength forces every closed door open and none of His plans return without being accomplished.

That is why we must recognise that even though the Bible is an open cheque book, it takes faith to draw from it. Moreover, among other benefits, faith confers us with supernatural mastery over life's situations and circumstances.

As it is written: ***For whatsoever is born of God overcometh the world: and this is the victory that overcometh the world, even our faith*** (1 John 5:4).

Therefore, until we understand the mystery of faith in the Word, our discovery from the Scriptures (revelation) will be mere frustration because it is faith that defines everyone's destiny. As Jesus once said: ***...According to your faith, be it unto you*** (Matthew 9:29).

In this end-time, the dramatic change of levels in the church will be so amazing that the world will marvel at it, but our faith is needed for these turnarounds to be actualised. It is impossible to experience supernatural turnaround except our faith is activated to receive what we have seen in the Scriptures. This is because our change of levels can be so drastic that except our faith is ready, we might be unable to accommodate it.

When God told me that it was time to get the aircraft, I heard Him clearly because it was not premeditated. I knew it was an avenue for a turnaround, and my faith accepted it without knowing the cost of the project. We need to build our faith in order to take delivery of our desired turnarounds. However, we must understand that faith comes from the Word; faith comes by hearing and understanding the Word (Romans 10:17).

We engage the Word of God to generate signs. In other words, every sign and wonder we see today is a confirmation of the Word. It is dangerous to take the Bible as our textbook, because we will never get anything from it. The Bible is a spiritual text and can only be accessed spiritually.

Throughout the building of the Faith Tabernacle, I never doubted once the possibility of its completion in one year. The truth is that, there was no opportunity to doubt because I understood that God is able to perform whatever He says. That is why it is important to build our faith or it will fail us when our lifting comes.

God's Word is pregnant with wonders and faith is what we use to release those wonders, because it is the answer to all impossibilities. Unquestionably, every lingering situation requiring an intervention is answerable only to faith because faith is a mountain mover. By faith, there is a solution to every issue that confronts us.

It is important to note that our understanding of the depth of the Word that relates to our circumstances is what determines the strength of our faith on that issue. That is, the clearer we see what the Word says about us, the stronger our faith. It is one thing to receive the Word, and another to believe it. A combination of the two is what empowers us for dominion. Faith is the live wire of the believer, while understanding gives life to our faith.

God has made provisions for our total health, prosperity, breakthroughs and turnarounds in the Scriptures, but our faith needs to come alive to receive them. That is why the Bible says without faith it is impossible to please God and if we cannot please Him, we cannot receive anything from Him. As it is written:

> ***But let him ask in faith, nothing wavering. For he that wavereth is like a wave of the sea driven with the wind and tossed. For let not that man think that he shall receive any thing of the Lord.***
>
> *James 1:6-7*

Furthermore, faith in the Word entails believing equally whatever we have received, which in turn empowers us to manifest as sons of God. Therefore, we must understand that what we hear is powerless until we believe it; and what we receive is helpless until we believe it. It is a combination of receiving and believing that empowers our full-scale manifestation. It is not enough to receive the Word, we must go a little further to believe the Word in order to dominate our circumstances (John 1:12).

The Nature of Faith

Faith is in Action, not in Words

Faith is doing what God says in His Word about any desire of our lives. Faith is the answer to all seemingly impossible situations around us. When our faith is released, it changes our status spiritually to make us operate in the heavenlies.

Every act of faith on the Word of God commits God's integrity to perform and when He steps in, marvels happen. When we encounter God's Word, it addresses any issue of our lives provided we act in faith; because that makes us commit God to bail us out of it. We must not assume that we believe because we are to consciously mix the Word with faith in our hearts. The Bible records that with the heart man believes, not with the head (Romans 10:10).

Every mighty act of God in the book of Exodus was the result of what God said to Moses; and it was not just what God said, but the instructions Moses acted on.

> ***He made known His ways unto Moses, His acts unto the children of Israel.***
>
> *Psalm 103:7*

So, God's Word was the gateway to His great acts in the life of Moses. God made His ways known to Moses and His ways generated His acts. Thus, when He said, "And thou shall take this rod in thy hand, wherewith thou shalt do signs...," God was talking about him taking His Word as He said it and by doing so, Moses commanded signs. When we take God's Word as He says it (raw) and act on it, He is committed to perform that Word in our lives (Exodus 4:17).

Understanding inspires faith, because it simply means being able to see what God is saying and that comes through a process of meditation. Meditation is pondering on the Word we have received in our hearts, till faith is secreted to absorb it. That is why we need to get hold of the right word to consciously release and activate our faith.

As it is written: ***So then faith cometh by hearing, and hearing by the word of God*** (Romans 10:17).

Faith is a Spiritual Force Within that Determines the Triumphs and Happenings Around Us

When the paralytic man was lowered through the roof, Jesus saw the force of faith within them and said, ***arise, and take up thy bed*** (Mark 2:9).

There was also a cripple that Paul perceived had faith to be healed and he commanded him to stand up. Immediately, he was made whole. The force of faith within created the environment for his healing and deliverance (Acts 14:9-10).

The level at which the Word will profit us is determined by the degree of faith within us. Therefore, faith is not on the face, but in the heart. The events of our lives are according to our faith. Every man's future is as designed by his faith. Therefore, it is wisdom to invest in our faith and keep it strong, so that when God unveils His next level plan for us, our faith can receive it.

As it is written: ***...According to your faith be it unto you*** (Matthew 9:29).

Faith is not a Dormant Force; it is a Dominant Force

When faith is at work on the inside, it dominates our environment. It is common knowledge that faith does not live under circumstances, it lives above them.

> ***And Elijah answered and said to the captain of fifty, if I be a man of God, then let fire come down from heaven, and consume thee and thy fifty. And there came down fire from heaven, and consumed him and his fifty.***
>
> *2 Kings 1:10*

Elijah dominated his environment by the authority he had through his faith in the Word of God. Therefore, faith dominates its environment and subdues kingdoms. Undoubtedly, the effect of faith is our dominion over situations and circumstances of life (Hebrews 11:33).

Before I started having children, satan said to me: "Now that you have gone about setting other people free from barrenness, let me see how you will have children." I replied, "You will be surprised that I won't pray about it."

That conversation was within, but I replied him in the strength of the authority of my faith. So, when my wife said she had a miscarriage, I said: "It cannot happen!" It was not premeditated or arranged, neither was I confessing scriptures, but I was dominating the environment. I said it and went to bed, and there was no prayer point on it.

When the Word of God illuminates us, we become "wild".

Faith is the Spiritual Virtue that Establishes Our Partnership with the Invincible God, thereby Empowering Us to do the Impossible

> ***What shall we then say to these things? If God be for us, who can be against us?***
>
> *Romans 8:31*

Moses' faith was strong, because he saw God as invincible, thereby commanding the impossible. Moses was in partnership with God by faith.

Every time our faith comes alive, God's partnership with us is established, to deal with the issues of life. With that, we can command the impossible when we believe in Him.

Paul said: ***For what if some did not believe? Shall their unbelief make the faith of God without effect? God forbid: yea, let God be true, but every man a liar; as it is written, That thou mightest be justified in thy sayings, and mightest overcome when thou art judged*** (Romans 3:3-4).

Faith establishes our partnership with God and makes us invincible, as seen in the case of the three Hebrew boys.

> ***Then Nebuchadnezzar spake, and said, Blessed be the God of Shadrach, Meshach, and Abed-nego, who hath sent his angel, and delivered his servants that trusted in him, and have changed the king's word, and yielded their bodies, that they might not serve nor worship any god, except their own God.***
>
> *Daniel 3:28*

For instance, Jesus was constantly with the Father and that made Him invincible. Also, when the Israelites believed God and moved towards the Red Sea, "the sea saw them and fled." Their partnership with God made them more than conquerors.

Faith is not Just Reaching Out to God, Who is in Heaven, it is Bringing Him Down to Where We are

His name is the Omnipotent God, and with the breath of His nostrils, He will slay His enemies. It is the faith of an individual that determines his ultimate placement.

Remember, it takes our faith to connect with the anointing. Anyone can connect with whatever his faith can catch; for it is to us, in the ultimate, according to our faith. Jesus, Who is the Resurrection and the Life, went to a little village and couldn't do any mighty work because there was no faith to connect with. Therefore, we must pay the required price towards building our faith (Matthew 9:29, 13:58).

> ***For Sarah conceived, and bare Abraham a son in his old age, at the set time of which God had spoken to him.***
>
> *Genesis 21:2*

However, our faith must not just capture the content; it must capture the timing. If God says "this time tomorrow," our faith must be alive to capture it, so we can operate in that realm.

We understand from the Scriptures that every prophetic agenda is for an appointed time, and it was recorded that Jesus wept over Jerusalem because they did not know the time of their visitation. Moreover, a prophetic agenda is what sets the stage for divine visitation. Therefore, we must be time conscious so that we don't miss our visitation for a turnaround (Habakkuk 2:1-3; Luke 19:41-44).

We must see ourselves from the eyes of the Scriptures. Remember, it is an individual's faith that guarantees the delivery of that individual's portion. Daniel's faith distinguished him in the midst of horror because he believed in his God. It was practically impossible to hurt him (Daniel 6:23).

There is also what to do to commit God to make good His promise in our lives. However, a discovery of what to do is called **revelation** and doing it is **faith**. Faith is not just about believing God, it is obeying God to prove that we believe Him so as to commit Him to make good His promise. That means there is always something to obey in order to provoke God's intervention in our lives.

Until we find what to do, we don't have revelation; we only have information. Information tells us what is available but it cannot deliver to us how to make it obtainable. It is revelation that entitles us to what is available. Thus, what is available is information but how to access it is revelation.

Note that faith is not cheap talk; it is hard work. For faith comes by hearing and hearing (understanding) the Word of God. It takes our depth of understanding to develop our faith to capture the things that God has in store. However, understanding is not cheap.

> ***Buy the truth, and sell it not; also wisdom, and instruction, and understanding.***
>
> *Proverbs 23:23*

Faith has to be bought, not wished. We buy with our time, high-level discipline and understanding. Spiritual understanding is boosted by fasting, discipline and prayer.

Faith also comes by hearing from God; and hearing from Him is not cheap. It calls for high-level spiritual sensitivity 24/7 because we can't tell when He will speak. John said, "I was in the Spirit on the Lord's day..." (Revelation 1:10).

The Bible also says:

> ***I will stand upon my watch, and set me upon the tower, and will watch to see what he will say unto me, and what I shall answer when I am reproved.***
>
> *Habakkuk 2:1*

To hear from God, we must go up to the "watchtower".

Rhema is the principal booster of faith because we cannot hear from God and still doubt Him. His voice swallows the voice of many waters; His voice will swallow every form of doubt. When God speaks, doubts die. The voice of God killed doubt in Abraham. He did not stagger at the promise of God, but was fully persuaded of what God had spoken, not what he read.

What God says is the greatest sustainer of a man in the midst of conflict. When we hear from God, we are supernaturally in command of the conflicts of life.

> ***But the natural man receiveth not the things of the Spirit of God: for they are foolishness unto him: neither can he know them, because they are spiritually discerned.***
>
> *1 Corinthians 2:14*

Therefore, we cannot be carnal if we want to hear from heaven; we must be truly spiritual. We can't be talking chaff on the street, deceiving and lying, and expect to hear from God. He doesn't talk to such people.

We must come out of the carnal realm and dwell in the spiritual, in order to connect with what the Spirit has in store.

> ***He that hath an ear, let him hear what the Spirit saith unto the churches.***
>
> *Revelation 3:6*

The Spirit of God will only communicate with our spirit. It is Spirit-to-Spirit, human-to-human, dog-to-dog, etc. We cannot be in the flesh and hear what the Spirit of God is saying. We must be men of the Spirit to truly begin to hear from God. Thus, rhema is not cheap; rhema answers to high-level spiritual discipline.

People who hear from God are not on the streets talking chaff all around town. They are not gossips; they are not busy bodies in other men's matters. Those who hear from God always package themselves in an intimate walk with God.

We labour to hear from God by studying and meditating on His Word and other anointed materials of proven men and women of God. Everything about faith requires a demanding input from us. It does not answer to wishes but workings. It's time to work it out. We do not have to watch any aspect of our lives go down the drain. Rather, we must reach out to work out our salvation. We cannot wait for our faith to develop itself, we must develop it. If we don't follow the steps, we cannot duplicate the results.

We must understand that our faith has an unlimited capacity to grow. However, the level of our faith limits our turnarounds. Revelation is the platform for this growth because it is spiritual understanding that builds faith. We cannot grow in faith by wishing, there are practical steps to growing in faith.

Build your faith to dominate anything that is yet to bow. If you are looking for a job, build your faith on the provision of a miracle job. I built my faith on church growth and kept building it, and the church has no choice but to keep growing.

I consciously developed my faith on finance until I dominated it. I also dominated sickness boldly and I have dominated death practically. Jesus has the key and He is holding the key in our favour, so how can death harass us? If the Spirit that raised Jesus from the dead dwells in us, that same Spirit will quicken our mortal bodies. It is impossible to come across any faith giant who is not a Word addict. Therefore, receive grace to build your faith in the Word, thereby commanding dominion over life's situations and circumstances in Jesus' name!

THIRTEEN

POWER OF HOPE

For there is hope of a tree, if it be cut down, that it will sprout again, and that the tender branch thereof will not cease. Though the root thereof wax old in the earth, and the stock thereof die in the ground; Yet through the scent of water it will bud, and bring forth boughs like a plant.

Job 14:7-9

From the above scripture, it is evident that there is no closed case with God. The only concluded case is the one we closed ourselves. It says, through the scent of water, which can be referred to as the Word as seen in Ephesians 5:26, there shall be a springing forth. Therefore, when it comes to engaging the Word of God for a turnaround, nothing can be termed impossible.

Abraham was 75 years old when the Word came:

> ***And I will make of thee a great nation, and I will bless thee, and make thy name great; and thou shalt be a blessing:***
>
> ***And I will bless them that bless thee, and curse him that curseth thee: and in thee shall all families of the earth be blessed.***
>
> *Genesis 12:2-3*

But it took 25 years before ***the LORD visited Sarah as He had said, and the Lord did unto Sarah as He had spoken. For Sarah conceived and bare Abraham a son in his old age, at the set time of which God had spoken to him*** (Genesis 21:1-2).

Still, he believed it and his faith engendered an automatic fulfilment of the Word.

Every spoken word guarantees the opening of a new chapter. No situation is too late for a turnaround. Lazarus was dead for four days, his body was already stinking and the whole family had given up on him. The situation seemed impossible, until Jesus intervened and Lazarus came back to life (John 11:21-40).

Martha said in verse 39 of that scripture that he (Lazarus) was already stinking. That meant, "Master, you are late!" Also, when Mary heard that the Master was around, she ran out to meet Him and repeated the same words; meaning, the situation was too late for a turnaround (John 11:21, 32).

But Jesus said, ***if thou wouldest believe, thou shouldest see the glory of God*** (John 11:40). Therefore, at any stage in our lives, when the Word comes, a turnaround comes. We need to have an understanding of how the Word operates, to boost our confidence in it.

Also, we must understand that God's Word is never late. It met Abraham at 75 and still produced, because God performed His Word. If God could speak a new beginning to Abraham at that age, our turnaround is sure at whatever level we are. All we need to do is to keep hunting for the word that will open up new chapters in our lives.

God said, ***if ye were Abraham's children, ye would do the works of Abraham*** (John 8:39).

God is never late! Taking another example from Zachariah, who was ministering in the holiest of all when an angel of the Lord appeared to him and said he would have a son. He asked, "How would that be?" since he was an old man and his wife had also passed the age of childbearing (Luke 1:12-20).

However, God was true to His Word and Elizabeth eventually conceived in her old age. Therefore, it does not matter how long the situation has been, what is certain is that God's Word is never late and at the appointed time, it shall speak (Habakkuk 2:3).

The Word has capacity to enforce a supernatural turnaround at any point in time. Job was greatly blessed in Job 1:1-13, but in chapter 2:1-10, he lost everything. His wife told him to, "Curse God and die" but he rebuked her. Later, when he encountered God's Word, he experienced a change of story (Job 42:10-12).

Furthermore, in Luke 5:1-10, the fishermen were already washing their nets because they had a fruitless day. Nevertheless, the Word came, "launch out into the deep." When they obeyed that command, they had the greatest harvest ever.

> ***And saw two ships standing by the lake: but the fishermen were gone out of them, and were washing their nets.***
>
> ***And he entered into one of the ships, which was Simon's, and prayed him that he would thrust out a little from the land. And he sat down, and taught the people out of the ship.***
>
> ***Now when he had left speaking, he said unto Simon, Launch out into the deep, and let down your nets for a draught.***
>
> ***And Simon answering said unto him, Master, we have toiled all the night, and have taken nothing:***

nevertheless at thy word I will let down the net.

And when they had this done, they inclosed a great multitude of fishes: and their net brake.

And they beckoned unto their partners, which were in the other ship, that they should come and help them. And they came, and filled both the ships, so that they began to sink.

Luke 5:2-7

By obedience to the word of command from Jesus, there was a supernatural, net-breaking and boat-sinking turnaround. Meanwhile, they had already resigned to fate before the Word brought a turnaround for them.

The Word can also make a "giant" out of a "dwarf". Gideon was the least in a very poor family. His father was the poorest in their tribe, which was the least among the tribes of Israel. Thus, he belonged to the least of the least order.

However, there came a word, ***thou mighty man of valour***, and a "giant" arose out of a "dwarf". God's Word can change anybody's story dramatically. That word sent to Gideon, through the angel of the Lord, gave the assurance that mighty men of valour can emerge out of weaklings (Judges 6:11-16, 25-37).

Similarly, the word turned Joseph's destiny around, even as a prisoner. The Word of the Lord has no regard for where you are or how terrible the situation is. When it is your time for a turnaround, it locates you, no matter where you are and as it meets you, your story is changed forever.

It was said of Joseph: ***Until the time that his word came: the word of the LORD tried him. The king sent and loosed him; even the ruler of the people, and let him go free. He made him lord of his house, and ruler of all his substance*** (Psalm 105:19-21).

We must understand that it is the Word sent to us concerning our situation that puts us in command of the issues of life. This is why until we access the Word, we do not qualify for a turnaround. We know that what we do not expect, we are not permitted to experience; because, faith is the substance of things expected and the evidence of things not seen.

I have said it so many times that I am not surprised at where we are now as a ministry, but I would have been surprised if we were not there. This is because faith gives substance to our expectations, which is the good ground for its (faith) manifestation. Therefore, without expectation, our faith remains impotent (Luke 1:45).

We must have the consciousness that if we do not believe the Word, it will never be fulfilled in our lives. We have to believe the Word concerning our turnaround before we can experience it.

Our Turnaround Requires Expectation

Everyone needs a change of level but expectation is God's wisdom for provoking our manifestation. As believers, we have a lifelong turnaround heritage in Christ, our Justifier before God.

However, we live in a Kingdom that operates on keys and expectation is one of the keys to receiving God's blessings.

> ***And I say also unto thee, That thou art Peter, and upon this rock I will build my church; and the gates of hell shall not prevail against it. And I will give unto thee the keys of the kingdom of heaven...***
>
> *Matthew 16:18-19*

A Word from the Lord is the key to our turnarounds. If we want to experience a turnaround, we must go after a Word from the Lord and expect to receive it.

God said, ***let there be light, and there was light*** (Genesis 1:3). God said, God saw and Genesis 1:31 further confirms that God saw everything that He said and behold, it was very good.

The good news is that God, Who created the entire world in six days, is still working. If by the Word, God reframed this world, that same God of six days will reframe your life in the name of Jesus!

FOURTEEN

TAKE IT BY FORCE

...work out your own salvation with fear and trembling.

Philippians 2:12

When we are driving towards set goals that we desperately want to accomplish, we always have the energy to be persistent. Without the desperation for a change, we may never take delivery of our desires. We must take appropriate steps to get our hearts' desires met.

Therefore, it takes personal responsibility to enforce a turnaround. Also, we must know that our hearts are the connection to the delivery of our desires because the desperation that we need comes from the heart.

It is written: ***...The effectual fervent prayer of a righteous man availeth much*** (James 5:16).

Our consistency, desperation and push in getting our desires is what brings them to manifestation. Thus, when our hearts are connected and we are desirous enough for a turnaround, God manifests Himself on our behalf. This is because without working out our desires, they may never materialise on their own.

> ***With my soul have I desired thee in the night; yea, with my spirit within me will I seek thee early: for when thy judgments are in the earth, the inhabitants of the world will learn righteousness.***
>
> *Isaiah 26:9*

However, it is important that we reposition ourselves to hear from the Lord. Bartimaeus heard that Jesus, the One Who heals the sick and raises the dead, was passing by and that prompted him to scream until he caught His attention (Mark 10:46-52).

God brought a turnaround to the entire creation in six days and there are four sets of six days in a month for us to enforce our desired turnarounds, by taking personal responsibility on the prayer altar. The earth was without form and void, darkness was upon the deep; but when God stepped in, He created all things in six days.

Then He said, ***the earth is the LORD's and the***

fulness thereof (Psalm 24:1).

Elijah was at the point of suicide when a wind came from the Lord in 1 Kings 19:8-17. God's Word came and opened a new chapter to him. Talking about Joseph, the Bible says: ***Until the time that his word came: the word of the LORD tried him.*** But when his word came, ***The king sent and loosed him...*** (Psalm 105:19-20). The king sent for him, loosed him, decorated him and gave him a place in the palace.

Do you know why Abraham was so strong? He operated with the Word from the Lord. The Bible says, ***the LORD had said unto Abram, Get thee out of thy country...*** (Genesis 12:1).

When we hear from the Lord, fear dies! This is because the voice of the Lord is mightier than the voice of many waters. Abraham ***staggered not at the promise of God through unbelief; but was strong in faith, giving glory to God; And, being fully persuaded that, what He had promised, He was able also to perform*** (Romans 4:17-21).

He knew that he had met with greatness because he heard it from God. Abraham was stable, steadfast and steady.

... according to that which was spoken, so shall thy seed be (Romans 4:18). We must operate with what has been spoken concerning us in the Scriptures, not by what we read somewhere.

Every time we hear from God, celebration begins. Abraham celebrated multitudes. However, we cannot celebrate except we access that which is spoken. A Word from the Lord is only accessible by the ministry of the Holy Spirit. He receives from the Lord and delivers it to us; He is the Mediator between the Father and us, His children.

As it is written:

> ***I have yet many things to say unto you, but ye cannot bear them now.***
>
> ***Howbeit when he, the Spirit of truth, is come, he will guide you into all truth: for he shall not speak of himself; but whatsoever he shall hear, that shall he speak: and he will shew you things to come.***
>
> ***He shall glorify me: for he shall receive of mine, and shall shew it unto you.***
>
> *John 16:12-14*

It is also written: ***...for the Spirit searcheth all things, yea, the deep things of God*** (1 Corinthians 2:10).

Our spirit-man must be actively alive to access a Word from the Lord because God is a Spirit and they that worship Him must do so in spirit and in truth. We can only connect with the Word through our spirit. God is Spirit and only spirits can hear Him (John 4:24).

The Spirit itself beareth witness with our spirit, that we are the children of God:

Romans 8:16

It is important that our spirit-man stays robustly alive, and we must stop playing religious politics. We need to stop junketing around because if we cannot hear from God, we cannot be in command, which means we cannot have the key to our breakthroughs. That, therefore, means we are bound to remain stranded.

Just as a dog hears dogs, human beings hear humans. To you, a dog is barking but to another dog, it is speaking. To you, a sheep is bleating but to another sheep, it is giving commands. In the same vein, only spirits can hear God! This is why our spirit-man must come alive!

When Adam's spirit died, he was disconnected from God and could not hear Him again. Similarly, until our spirit-man bounces back to real vital life, we cannot hear from God.

Therefore, we must take responsibility to hear from God constantly in order to see that we actualise our turnarounds. By taking responsibility, we must crave, thirst and plug into every Word from God. This is because every statement of the Scripture is prophetic and God does not direct His Words to any specific group, but to all who care to take the Word seriously. Therefore, receive the grace to diligently seek your turnaround Word and as you do, I decree that every turnaround you desire come to manifestation in Jesus' name!

ABOUT THE *Author*

David O. Oyedepo, called to be an Apostle with a mandate to liberate the world through the preaching of the Word of Faith, has for nearly four decades been part of the ongoing charismatic revival sweeping across the African continent today. His faith-based teachings have literarily transformed millions of lives around the world.

He is the Founder and President of the Living Faith Church Worldwide also known as Winners' Chapel International, with a network of thousands of Churches in Nigeria and several other nations across the continents of the world.

Till date, he has published over 90 impactful titles most of which have been translated to major languages of the world such as French, Chinese, Spanish etc. with over twenty million copies in circulation.

He is the Senior Pastor of the Faith Tabernacle, Canaanland, Ota, Nigeria, with a 50,000-seat sanctuary, reputed to be the largest church facility in the world. The church currently runs five services on Sunday morning with over 300,000 worshippers, making her one of the largest church congregations in the world.

His mission has established educational institutions across all levels in Nigeria, with Covenant and Landmark Universities taking large strides towards becoming world class universities.

He is married to Faith and they are blessed with sons, daughters and grandchildren.

Books By Dr David Oyedepo

- Not By Power Nor By Might
- The Turnaround Power Of The Word
- Understanding The Power Of Faith
- The Breakthrough Power Of Vision
- On Eagle's Wings
- The Unlimited Power Of Faith
- In Pursuit Of Vision
- Pillars Of Destiny
- Signs & Wonders Today
- Exploits In Ministry
- Winning The War Against Poverty
- Walking In Dominion
- Possessing Your Possession
- The Wisdom That Works
- Exploits Of Faith
- Anointing For Exploits
- Understanding The Power Of Praise
- Walking In Newness Of Life
- Maximise Destiny
- Commanding The Supernatural
- Winning Invisible Battles
- Success Systems
- Understanding Financial Prosperity
- Success Strategies
- Understanding Your Covenant Right
- Miracle Meal
- Exploring the Riches of Redemption
- Anointing For Breakthrough
- Excellency Of Wisdom
- Breaking Financial Hardship
- The Release Of Power
- Walking In The Miraculous

Books By Dr David Oyedepo

- Satan Get Lost!
- The Winning Wisdom
- Walking In Wisdom
- The Healing Balm
- Manifestations Of The Spirit
- Breaking The Curses Of Life
- Overcoming Forces Of Wickedness
- You Shall Not Be Barren!
- Exploring The Secrets Of Success
- Winning Prayer
- Understanding The Anointing
- Fulfilling Your Days
- Towards Mental Exploits
- Understanding Vision
- Understanding Divine Direction
- The Force Of Freedom
- Born To Win
- The Shower Of Blessing
- Riding On Prophetic Wings
- All You Need To Have All Your needs Met
- Operating In The Supernatural
- Ruling Your World
- The Blood Triumph
- Keys To Divine Health
- Winning Faith
- Conquering Controlling Powers
- Put Your Angels To Work
- Covenant Wealth
- Keys To Answered Prayer
- Miracle Seed
- The Hidden Covenant Of Blessing

INSIDE VIEW OF
Faith Tabernacle

Dr David Oyedepo is the Founding President of the Living Faith Church Worldwide Inc. and the Senior Pastor of the Faith Tabernacle, a 50,000 capacity sanctuary located in Canaanland, Ota, a suburb of Lagos, Nigeria.

The construction of this gigantic architectural masterpiece was completed within twelve months and dedicated on September 18, 1999, built totally debt-free and without any foreign inputs! To God alone be all the glory.

Today, Faith Tabernacle stands as the home of signs and wonders for men and women all over the world, who keep coming in droves to worship the King of kings and the Lord of lords, Jesus Christ the Son of the Living God.

OUTSIDE VIEW OF FAITH TABERNACLE

OVERVIEW OF FAITH TABERNACLE

Visit our website for more information: www.faithtabernacle.org.ng

Some Facilities at Covenant University

African Leadership Development Centre

4,000-Seat University Chapel

Post Graduate Halls Of Residence

Some Facilities at Landmark University

University Library

University Chapel

Students' Hall Of Residence